ASCEND

the

DEPTH

RIGHTEOUS RISE

AKBAR JAFFARI Ph.D.

ASCEND THE DEPTH
RIGHTEOUS RISE

iUniverse books may be ordered through booksellers or by contacting:

iUniverse
1663 Liberty Drive
Bloomington, IN 47403
www.iuniverse.com
844-349-9409

ISBN: 978-1-6632-5470-2 (sc)
ISBN: 978-1-6632-5469-6 (e)

Library of Congress Control Number: 2023913128

Print information available on the last page.

iUniverse rev. date: 12/22/2023

ABOUT THE BOOK

This book is a journey of human perversion from its innate qualities of peace and happiness, towards living a most sophisticated unrelated, fictitious, and atrocious life, that has bread widespread and intense pains and agonies. It travels through 80 thousand years of humans' lost directions and instructions. It searches through multiple root causes of human disidentification with real selves and innate qualities. The book has good news that salvation is real and has started. The book provides real practical approaches to firstly, return to the true self and live in peace and harmony, and secondly, take part in the return journey of reconnecting with the divine forces, and allowing the universe to manifest its purposes. The journey is a work in progress, may take time for the collective humanity to awaken and regain its consciousness, fortunately, as the book guides, the first step is itself a big step that can and will disseminate impactful and tangible realization and consciousness.

The journey may become blissful disguised in pain for some. For others it turns, as is the case with increasingly more people all over the world, to be a natural inner self tendency toward dissociating with the fictitious and malicious self. The unique approach of the book is that it resolves human dysfunctions, in real-life situations, divorced from any rituals or sugar-coated environment.

The book's main objective is to diffuse the inherited behavioral layers of individuals and collective societies and reach the depth of the Divine source of righteousness for serving the universe and the wellbeing of Mankind. The journey has no detour once it starts .Your job is to start the journey.

TABLE OF CONTENTS

ACKNOWLEDGMENTS

Firstly, I would like to thank Dr. Abdul Hussain Mirza for his valuable comments and suggestions he made on the original manuscript. He greatly enriched the value of the book and made it more beneficial.

I extend my gratitude to Mr. Ahmad Albahar for his in-depth critique of the facts and concepts demonstrated in the book. His intervention contributed greater understanding of the most challenging connotations.

I am also thankful to Mr. Mohammed Kamal for his highly intellectual and informative debates, which led to more consolidation of the notions and paraphrasing of selected narratives.

I am deeply grateful to my colleague Mr. Jalal Majeed for his assistance in editing the text and designing the structure of the format of the book.

I am especially thankful to Ms. Fatima Burashid, who prompted the initial suggestion that inspired me to transform the knowledge into this book.

I am profoundly grateful to Ms. Annabelle Mendez, senior publishing consultant, at iUniverse Publishing company, for delicately processing publishing activities, with great commitment, care and cheer.

My love and appreciation go to those, particularly the young, who attended my speeches and inspired me to document and compile them in this book.

Finally, I remain indebted to my wife, Khadija, for her love, companionship, and care and my sons, Ahmad and Jalal, for their understanding and support.

Above all, I would like to express my gratitude to the losses and challenges I encountered during my life, without which this book would not have been actualized.

INTRODUCTION

The recorded history of mankind spans twelve thousand years. Throughout this long period, there has not been a day without conflicts, wars, and atrocities among humans. Russian writer Fyodor Dostoyevsky said, "I do not appreciate the history of the world; it is the records of human insanity, no more." Former British prime minister Winston Churchill once impulsively said that history is "one damn thing after another." During your lifetime, do you know of any one day when humanity was in total peace and serenity? You may wish to search through your memories or references, but rest assured you will not find one.

All religions, philosophies, and spiritual teachings confirm that the innate and inherent qualities of mankind are peace, love, and happiness. These qualities contravene human behavioral legacies. It is impossible to accept both facets of human reality. As such, it is inconceivable to submit that the good quality of innate human tendencies produces atrocities and savageness. The reverse is equally true. Then what is causing such a painful controversy that has obscured and eclipsed humanity for thousands of years?

There must be an ulterior element instigating dysfunctional human behavior. I have been searching for this element since childhood. I went through emotional distress due to my childhood living condition, which was far less than a normal childhood life. Along the way, I came across numerous realities, facts, and enigmas.

The search never ends, as the ultimate truth remains infinite; however, I have found that the ulterior element disturbing human behavior and well-being is not the human him- or herself but the separate self.

I started talking about the separate self to individuals; gave speeches and press interviews; and was asked by establishments, both private and public, to incorporate the concept and mechanism of it into their work environment for productivity, profitability, and jubilation.

As time went on, people I spoke to started to suggest I document what I shared with them. It took me some time to reach a mind mode to start writing, as I have a full-time job managing a management consultancy firm. Finally, in March 2023, I managed to devote my full attention and time to writing this book.

I have not provided, in this section or anywhere in the book, an abstract of the book or summaries of the chapters, in order to avoid any preemptive assumption or the provocation of any dogma. No two people will read and understand this book the same way. I invite you to read or study this book in exactly the way that benefits you, avoiding any external influence on your understanding. You may challenge some parts or even the whole book. If you do, then you have found the ulterior element that is instigating emotional upheaval. If you don't, then you are already awakened. The book will share with you the functionalities of the ulterior element, and over time, you will observe it. When you do, then you don't observe it any longer, as it dissolves, paving the way for your innate qualities to manifest in peace, love, and happiness.

CHAPTER 1

DETOUR OF THE HUMAN JOURNEY

IN QUEST OF PURPOSE

LIFE IS INHERENTLY MYSTERIOUS, TROUBLESOME, and ambiguous, as we do not understand our relationship with the world we live in and our purpose among billions of creatures and galaxies. You may have asked yourself, "Why am I here in this world?"

We are innately suspicious of any kind of answers we may give or receive. This is so because almost all replies are ambiguous and tantamount to beliefs that offer more ambiguity in our quest for the meaning of our existence in this world. Beliefs cannot offer any absolute, tangible, and realistic answers to anything.

We normally believe what we do not know. Conversely, if we know, then we do not believe. If I say, "I believe there are people in the next room," the listener will read that I do not know or, at best, am not sure, and obviously, he or she will not act on the information. Then the offer of information is not useful and can be misleading. In this context, beliefs not only are incapable of satisfying our quest for the truth but also probably will mislead us to potentially damaging consequences. Believing is, invariably, responding with conviction to dogmas and teachings we cannot comprehend. People tend to cling to what they do not know much more intensely than to what they know. For this reason, they are prepared to sacrifice their lives for causes they are is thinking constructive and veracious, and you use it when you need it and protect it against any misuse when it's not in your conscious use.

Conventional thinking cannot be positive by default, as much as we cannot claim warm ice. So we have either negative thinking or conscious use of the mind. You do not think; thinking is done to you by the ego.

This phenomenon is responsible for almost all human tragedies. When the mind produces thoughts, they are almost always negative thoughts that lead to negative emotions, negative actions, and psychological and physical pain and agonies. The mechanism that produces such fictitious and factitious mind-body interaction is called *ego*. I will explain the ego with a more in-depth illustration, as it is the vital and governing factor in our lives.

THE FALSE SELF

The ego is your false self. It is active and is maliciously fictitious yet viciously influential. The ego resembles software that acts as a disguised delivery server living in your body. It is full of negative energies and thoughts that are readily available to be triggered and activated for irrational purposes. It picks up negative, painful, tragic, and other unpleasant events and experiences accumulated in your life and saved in your memories—Sadhguru calls it "society's garbage bin"—only to retrieve them for you in times when you are least conscious of the motives, in order to make you relieve the agonies of the past or perceived future. When the ego pushes you into the future, you experience anxiety, and when it pulls you back into the past, you experience depression. In both cases, the degree of the emotional disturbances is relative to the intensity of the content of the thoughts.

MEMORY LAYERS

The ego, as a disguised delivery server, is one issue; the other issue involves your accumulated memories (society's garbage bin). Where do they come from? Are they all garbage?

There are four time-based sources of the memories we hold. The first and major source is the genetic source, which is transferred to us at the moment when the embryo is conceived in the womb and continues during the incubation period. Sources report that 20 percent to 60 percent of memory is inherited from past ancestors. An average of 40 percent of genetic memory is accepted for practical purposes. The other sources are childhood until the age of seven, adolescence until the age of twenty-three, and adulthood beyond the age of twenty-three. For these three stages, there are no empirical shreds of evidence suggesting the percentage volume of the memories we are holding. However, a consensus of scientific opinions suggests 25 percent for childhood memories,15 percent for adolescence, and 10 percent for adulthood.

In a normal mental condition, we are totally unaware of the genetic memory dynamics and hardly aware of the childhood memory but partially aware of the learned adolescent tendencies and perplexingly aware of the memories we gather during adulthood.

MEMORY FORMATION

No one can understand exactly how, technically, the genetic memories are formed and transferred to us. The childhood memories are transferred to us involuntarily as we are in a state of regressive hypnotism during the childhood period and learn under a state of total surrender. When a child reaches adolescence, he is voluntarily receptive to the environment and believes what is happening in his surroundings, and he must adopt social norms, or he will be out of the herd. So he goes on mimicking behaviors and habits through repetition. That is why we see most crowd gatherings, whether in sports events, demonstrations, riots, or even charity events, of this age group. Most are not properly aware of the subject matter. Toward the end of adolescence, the person starts to evaluate his adopted beliefs, tendencies, and behaviors and starts to shape his personality. Then he is out in the world on his own, only to face the thick walls of his legacies, compounded by the widespread irrationality of others.

Humans have an infinite memory capacity. It is utilized from the moment of inception in the womb until death. Much of the information is involuntarily stored in the memory, in biochemical form.

All memories are naturally neutral like other resources, not good or bad, but our reaction to them makes them so. Even tragic memory is not bad in the context of its independence and in isolation of any interaction with other components, nor is pleasant memory, for the same reason. German philosopher Arthur Schopenhauer affirms that no same external events or circumstances affect two people alike, even in perfectly similar surroundings. The mind carries incredible possibilities for imagination that have evolved over millions of years.

LIFE COMPONENTS

In parallel to the accumulation of memories from external sources, there is a source that provides us with the necessary information or packages of functional components in genetic memory to satisfy our needs to live conveniently and purposefully. Those components come with us as part of our body-and-mind configuration for all we need for our survival in this world. Most of the major religions and spiritual teachings have mentioned this phenomenon, albeit in a highly dogmatic manner, confirming that mankind is created in the best mold and the noblest image. The Brahma Kumaris, Indian spiritual teachings, specify seven such functional operating components that satisfy human living needs, which are similar to the hard disk operating software in your computer. These are happiness, love, peace, knowledge, wisdom, purity or clarity, and strength or power. Rumi, the thirteenth-century Persian philosopher, poet, and Sufi mystic, said that what you seek is already in you and is seeking you too, so make a way to reach it. These memory packages are strictly positive, with constructive intents and purposes in life. These function as software and respond to the purposes of the universe.

EVIL AND GOOD

The two parallel drives—the memories and life components—are in constant conflict. The memory drives through ego, and life components drive through divine conscious will. This is the struggle between evil and good that stranded mankind ever since the ego gained access to the mind.

The ego tries ceaselessly to sever the communication between the mind and the life components by occupying the mind and influencing it to produce false and fictitious thoughts and emotions based on the triggers it receives from external life situations through the five senses. The ego thrives on these conditions; it gains more power over your mind, and if you react to the ego's motions, it will occupy your mind more intensely and for longer periods. During the periods of ego's dwelling in your mind, you are barred from reaching the life components, which are the source of your well-being. Ego's function is to tap into your memory and retrieve information to set a scene of life for you that is fictitious and tantalizing.

BEING IN THE MIND

Early man was free of the ego and was in total harmony with his inner self and his surroundings. Today man is somewhat paralyzed and enslaved by the ego's constant derangements and mischiefs, which puts him in a state of varying degrees of unconsciousness. Consequently, humanity is, unfortunately, living a marginal life condition. Most people cannot realize their potential; they are barred from reality, which is masked by the ego. Eckhart Tolle suggests that when you meet people on the streets, in workplaces, in schools, and in other places, most of them are not mentally in the places they are in. Their minds are either in the place they have come from, thinking about what they said, what they did, what they should have said, and what they should have done, or in the place they are going to, thinking about what to say, what to do, and what others might say or do and probably thinking about other people or things in those places in the same manner. Whatever the mind is engaged with is not in the present time and place, except for the awareness of not bumping into others or physical items. In such situations, ego is at work, gaining momentum and being nourished for the next round, which is imminent.

INQUISITIVE TOURIST

An exception is found in the people who deliberately want to be in a place for the sake of it or to see things and meet people as an endeavor to learn or discover certain knowledge, as in the case of tourists, explorers, researchers, or anyone on an inquisitive mission. What makes these latter people, or their minds, be where they are and not be as former people somewhere else are their conscious observation and attention to their surroundings.

Storing of memory is mostly done involuntarily, like autosave on your computer, unless you consciously intervene, as in the case of the latter people. They use their minds to interact with items, physical or otherwise, in front of them or voluntarily think about them. This is a great way to use the mind and not let the mind use you and is an effective way to combat the ego and bar it from using the mind.

SENSE PERCEPTION

This motion is called sense perception, or sense observation, in both scientific and spiritual terms. It can be used anywhere, at any time, and for any length of time, particularly when the ego occupies your mind. You can pick up anything in front of you and look at it with focus, staying there for three to five minutes. If you enjoy doing it, continue if you wish. If you can, get closer to the item, twenty to twenty-five centimeters. Any item you choose will work to engage your mind voluntarily. However, better items are those that are living beings, such as trees, flowers, plants, and even pets or toddlers. Paintings, embroideries, and craftworks are also items of power to engage your mind. In all cases, just look around intentionally at things near you. If you are in your sitting room, look at pieces of furniture, the curtains, the carpet, and the TV set, and insist on staying with your mind in that room or place. After a reasonably extended period of focusing on any item, particularly a living being, you start to sense a growing relationship with the item and then, eventually, feel you are part of it, or it is part of you. This is because the life (soul) running through you and through it is the same life, and you are both emanations of the same source of life, which is the source of the universe. This is the basic definition of *love*.

If your mind takes you out of the place you are in, then the ego is using your mind. The highest levels of sense perceptions are practiced by yogis in India and elsewhere in the East, where they stay rigidly still for long hours. Sense perception is one of many elements of spiritual practices and yoga. It is important to realize that we, as people going through our normal lives, do not in any way need to plunge into hardcore spiritual and yoga practices. What we need to improve our wellbeing and alleviate ego-induced pains and agonies is no more than what I described earlier: coming to the present time and becoming conscious of our mind and self.

CONSCIOUS BREATHING

Another hands-on tool you can use is conscious breathing. This type of breathing is different from normal breathing. Normal breathing is involuntary and is the minimum breathing you need to stay alive. Mostly, you are not aware of it. Conscious breathing is deliberate, and you are aware of it fully; you should feel the air enter your nostril passages, your throat, and then your lungs.

Put your attention fully on the air you are breathing. Slowly start breathing deeper and deeper but not forcefully. Stay conscious of the flow of the air throughout your respiratory passage. Breathe ten times, and you will inevitably feel your mind easing. This is when your mind starts creating space and forcing out egoic thoughts. Breathing reduces or stops thinking. Eckhart Tolle ascertains that breathing and thinking cannot happen at the same time. Your objective in this exercise is to reduce or stop thinking.

You can perform conscious breathing anywhere and anytime. It does not require prior arrangements or rituals, as practiced by members of spiritual communities or yogis, although they are profoundly useful. Conscious breathing is your potent weapon to combat the ego's interference with your mind. Exercise it whenever and wherever you face a challenging life situation or are attacked by fear, anxiety, emotional discomfort, depression, or any distressful feelings.

Sensory perception and conscious breathing exercises are specifically devised to help you in challenging day-to-day life situations; they are not confined to mountaintops, temples, or any dedicated places, nor do you need to shave your head or wear a saffron robe and glean food on the streets. However, practicing in these locations and adhering to their rituals can enforce your skills and prepare you more for real-life situational responses and performances.

Meditation involves one breath in and one breath out, as Eckhart Tolle mentions repeatedly. Conscious breathing while looking at a flower is a more profound meditation. In this meditative condition, you are conscious of your mind and aware of the ego play in the now. In any other condition, the ego pulls you below conscious level, which conjures irrationality into your behavior.

CHAPTER 3

THE IRRATIONALITY
OF THE MIND

GOING ASTRAY

THE ROOT OF ALL OUR suffering lies in not being in the present time, the now. Ego, through your accumulated memories and the external triggers you offer it, thrives on taking you out of the now and into the past or the future. Neither exists in reality, yet they cause massive disruption to your life, inducing irrationality in your behavior. Sadly, we are all on the irrationality spectrum. Some are high up, and some are low down, but no one is free of it. A vast number of people live in states of constant anxiety and depression. Some are suffering from their failures, but ironically, many are suffering from the consequences of their success. Some are agitated by their limitations, but many are restless about their freedom. When you are hungry, you have one serious problem; when you have a full stomach, you have multiple problems.

Most people go through the entire day without a glimpse of bliss; they are not without a single moment of distaste, anxiety, fear, irritation, despondency, confusion, and inferiority. There is nothing in this world that has the essence to cause such human suffering, not even natural disasters, such as earthquakes and hurricanes, which do not ever intentionally target human beings. Sadhguru, in one of his classes, was asked by a lady why there are so many problems in the world. His reply came as a snow wash: "There is only one problem in the world,

DISBELIEVING BELIEFS

The moment you start seeking the truth, you start disbelieving the beliefs suggested and handed over to you by the ego. When you believe, you imply you do not know, as mentioned earlier. When you seek, you know you do not know but want to know. Without the right awareness and wisdom, walking the path of belief—worse still, with devotion—will surely lead to a delusional life, denial of the truth, and stagnation of life. Devotion to the truth, on the other hand, is assuring, offers ecstasy in life, and enables us to realize our potential and serve the purpose of the universe.

Awareness begins with knowing the source of the thought, which is triggered primarily by the ego. Usually, if a thought is triggered that leads to emotional disturbance and possible verbal or physical assault, you will assess the situation when the heat is over, in a few minutes, hours, days, or even months. The thought eventually disappears, and you come, as we say, to your senses. You probably regret it, feel wistful and pitiful, and say to yourself, "I do not know why I did that, and it was not worth it at all."

If you do not know why you behaved irrationally, the source of the thought is genetic. If you can somehow sense any relationship with your past, the thought probably is related to your childhood memory, which, in most cases, is unconscious and unclear but can be analyzed and related to specific childhood incidents or experiences that have lingered with you for some time, such as abuse, deprivation, abandonment, or even close protection and enmeshment. If the thought is triggered in your adolescence period, then your reaction is mostly less intense and vaguely explainable, but still, it is at the unconscious level. Finally, if your incident is related to your recent time, the adulthood period, your reaction is somewhat calculated, less hasty, and less aggressive yet still irrational, albeit with less intensity. As we progress in life, adulthood's reactions reduce progressively. That is when we call a person mature or wise.

MEMORY IS NEUTRAL

All memories are unreal and saved in a biochemical form. They are not good not bad. They can be harmful if they are triggered by the ego and useful if they are retrieved consciously by you through your mind. Some of them are dormant, and others are on the surface. Triggering, or retrieving, the information depends on the power of the calling. I do not wish to indulge in intricate scientific or spiritual teachings, but allow me here to discuss some facts and figures that may help you to understand the memory structure. By no means do they need to be fully understood or remembered.

Memories are unreal because they do not exist in physical form; you cannot see them, touch them, or sense them through any of the five senses. You interact with memories only through the mind by the influence of the ego or by your conscious calling. They serve the delutional intention of the ego or constructive purposes of the conscious development needed for improving life. In both cases, we are puzzled by the fact that we do not know exactly where memories are stored and how best we can avoid or make use of them.

MEMORY STORAGE

A speech sitting brought together Eckhart Tolle; Deepak Chopra, Indian American author of spiritual alternative medicine; and Wayne Dyer, American self-help author and spiritual teacher. It was before the COVID outbreak. On his turn, Chopra mentioned he had attended a conference that gathered 150 of the best neuroscientists. During deliberation, Chopra asked the neuroscientists where in the brain memory was stored, and Chopra received no answer, confirming that it was not in the brain.

US CBC Radio reported on October 16, 2022, that Anne Marie, at age fifty, had a heart transplant. But shortly after her heart transplant, something changed—something she could not easily explain. Anne Marie said, "I know I love my family, but I do not get that squishy feeling anymore." Thoughts and memories of her loved ones used to feel warm and tingly, she said. Now they felt logical or factual or cold. She loved her husband and did not know why she could not get the same feeling anymore. It was a loss to her, as she was a heart and relationship person. She continued asking why she could not feel that anymore.

In another case, Clair had a heart transplant. She reported after the transplant that she felt as if a second soul were sharing her body. She experienced an appetite for beer and junk food. Five months after the surgery, she dreamed about a tall man named Tim. Clair said she had warm and affectionate physical intimacy with Tim in the dream and felt they would be together forever. When she woke up, she was certain that Tim was the donor and that some part of his spirit and personality was in her. Later, she discovered her donor's identity and address. Eventually, she visited Tim's family. Their description of Tim matched the man she had seen in her dream.

These cases are seemingly rare but not unheard of. Some researchers believe it may be possible for donor organs to hold and even pass on the characteristics and experiences of their original owners to the new recipients via a process known as cellular memory transfer.

While the phenomena are not broadly consolidated, it is discussed that certain thoughts or emotions are stored in the cells of certain parts of the body, which are consequently affected by them. Nevertheless, the connection between our minds and our bodies is often treated as make-believe and mired in controversies among researchers. Drawing from research conducted in different countries, we look at which organs may be impacted by the emotions of joy, anger, grief, fear, and pensiveness.

Chinese medicine suggests the heart may be associated with feelings of joy and excitement when referring to agitation and overstimulation. Excitement can cause insomnia, agitation, and heart palpitations.

The emotion of anger is associated with a choleric tumor and causes resentment and irritability. It is believed that this emotion is stored in the liver and the gall bladder, which contains bile. Anger can cause headaches and hypertension, which can in turn affect the stomach and the spleen.

The emotion of grief is known to affect the lungs as well as the large intestine. These emotions can cause fatigue, shortness of breath, or ulcerative colitis.

The emotion of fear, if felt too deeply and for prolonged periods, can begin to affect the kidneys in a harmful way. This explains the urge to urinate when frightened, particularly in children.

The emotion of pensiveness is associated with a strenuous thought process that can drain your energy and lead to disharmony. This melancholic emotion is known to affect your spleen and can cause lethargy and lack of concentration.

Additional reports suggest that eczema is related to emotions developed during childhood due to abandonment experienced by the child, and people with chronic sinusitis are more likely to develop depression or anxiety.

Those with the worst symptoms are the most likely to experience mental health problems.

MIND-BODY RECIPROCAL INFLUENCE

Most cultures of the world have sayings that suggest which thought-induced emotions affect which body parts or organs carrying the relevant cells. Some of these sayings include "This news rumbled my stomach," "The incident broke my back," "Your decision sent a shiver down my spine" "The result blew my mind" "The situation is killing my appetite," and "Your talk is suffocating."

Both medical and cultural contexts indicate that the effect of mind over body and vice versa is seemingly proven, and it is essential to understand it in a broader sense.

Every part of our body and mind thrives on cells and their healthy functioning. There are up to about one hundred trillion cells of two hundred types vibrating simultaneously and carrying 1.4 volts each. Each cell is aware of the rest of the cells and communicates with them continuously. Every minute, nearly three hundred million cells die, which assimilate into the stream of life that keeps the body functioning. The cells uphold our genes, our DNA. Genes provide cells with instructions on how to function. DNA is the genetic material that contains plans for the design of living beings and is used to store data created by living things. If you were to uncoil each strand of DNA and place the strands end to end, the resulting strand would be 108 billion kilometers long, the same as about 150,000 round trips to the moon.

The information stored in the DNA is at four levels of your life stages and can be transferred to your biological successors. This information is stored in your DNA in biochemical codes, which are tinier than binary codes.

The information, in the form of memories, can be both accumulated and retrieved. Storing of memory is mostly done involuntarily, like autosave on your computer, unless you consciously intervene and delete. Retrieval of memory is the big issue that may help or hinder our lives. It helps if we retrieve and process the information in our mind consciously, which can create brilliant ideas, advancement, solutions, inventions, and remedies to improve life and bring us much comfort and convenience. The most unfortunate condition that happened to humans was the birth of the ego by overwhelming the mind with incessant thoughts that caused massive disruption to the awareness and conscious use of the mind.

Your mind is mostly occupied by a vicious user, the ego, which sends and retrieves memories from genes in your cells in destructive plays. The ego play, apart from causing you psychological upheavals, either de-energizes your cells or overenergizes them. Each cell is responsible for holding certain types of memories. The ego targets a cell to de-energize by using thoughts that induce regrets, sorrow, guilt, self-pity, hate, despondency, and shame, which create inactivity and depression. These are the memories related to your past. Ego overenergizes a cell by using thoughts causing fear, anxiety, lust, and uncertainty, which create stiffness and restlessness. That is your perceived memory of the future.

The ego de-energizes or overenergizes memory cells by lowering or raising the cells' voltage, which is set at 1.4 volts. Once the cells' voltage is tampered with by the ego, the synchronicity of the vibration of the cells and the dance of life are lost.

ENERGIZING AND DE-ENERGIZING THE CELLS

When a cell is de-energized by the ego, it becomes deficient in holding on to the information responsible for immunizing your body against certain diseases and is disabled in responding effectively to your conscious thought callings, shrinking inwardly, causing disruptions to other cells, rendering them inefficient, and creating compounded immunity deficiency and mental disturbances. People faced with this condition usually, depending on the intensity of it, are depressed, withdrawn, and frequently ill; walk hesitantly; are submissive; have bent spines and inward-curving shoulders and chests; lack vigor in their voices and talk; have difficulty in breathing; and turn into deeply passive, introverted personalities.

When a cell is overenergized by the ego, it becomes excessively vigorous in holding to itself, grows aggressively, and does not know when and how to renew itself. It grows atrociously, causing massive disruption to other cells, spreading inefficiencies among all the cells around it or related to it, and creating multiple physical and mental illness conditions. A cancer cell is one such cell.

People who experience this condition—again, depending on the intensity of it—suffer from high blood pressure, high sugar levels, and high IgE levels; are prone to other chronic diseases; are overly anxious, obsessively overactive, confused, sociopathic, and offensive; and turn into deeply passive, extroverted personalities.

We are all prone to all types of physical and mental diseases; no one can escape this fact, and we all have the right cells that can cause or avoid these diseases. What calls them to respond either way is your thought. What generates thought is either your conscious use of the mind or the ego. It is true, as repeatedly suggested by psychologists and spiritual practitioners, that all our diseases stem from our egoic thoughts, and conversely, all the remedies are affected by our conscious-focused thoughts of suggestibility.

Egoic thoughts can create a series of varying degrees of life-troubling diseases and serious, life-threatening, malignant, and chronic diseases. Luckily, all these diseases can also be remedied by proper conscious-focused thoughts. What is caused by thoughts can be obliterated by thoughts.

The mind-body conditions, apart from causing massive disruption to our lives at the physical level, affect the attitude that leads us to form behaviors that can have widespread dire consequences on ourselves and those around us.

ATTITUDE

Attitude involves the mind's predispositions, the source of which are the memories of certain ideas, values, people, systems, and institutions. It is vastly shaped by past experiences in life and upbringing. It is settled and relatively solid; however, it can be improved by conscious intervention or worsened by incessant thoughts. It influences behavior directly and wholly. It is the feedstock of the behavior. Behavior relates to the expression of feelings, actions, or inactions, orally and through silent expressions, as in body language. Good and bad behaviors stem from good and bad attitudes. The reverse is only marginally true for conscious intervention by reviewing, correcting, and repeating certain favored behaviors or by unconscious, compulsive tendencies, which are bound to make the matter worse.

PERSONALITY

Personality is another component of our conduct in a real-life situation. It is a controlled part of your behavior that, normally, you do not want to fully show or expose. It is based on how you want to be seen by others. The personality is yours, based on your background and upbringing, but it is for others. In a controlled manner, it is the way you behave and perform to suit your surroundings and conform with the cultural and social norms and laws. No one can be his or her real self anywhere and anytime except in intensively meditative condition. The *person* in *personality* indicates that it is not you. The word is derived from the Latin word *persona*, which means "mask" or "false self." The world itself is a false place, which requires us to act more than behave in full reality. That would be like dumping your junk onto people and surroundings. Shakespeare wrote that the world is a stage, and we are all actors. It is not bad to control your behavior and adjust it to suit the people and environment around you. On the contrary, it is wise to do so—but only if you use it for good and constructive purposes. It is harmful when acting is performed for malignant purposes, which most do, intentionally or unconsciously.

YOU ARE NEVER ALONE IN THIS WORLD

When you wake up from your sleep, it takes you only a few seconds to be with your false self, which starts talking to you and conducting your thoughts and activities. Then you go to the wider world. You inevitably must deal with other people, who probably stir up difficulties and make your time miserable, and possibly you do the same to them. One agonizing environment people encounter is the workplace.

CHAPTER 4

―― ⟋ ――

WORKPLACE

════════════════════

A COMMON PLACE, AMONG MANY PLACES, where people experience emotional upheaval and physical exhaustion nowadays is the workplace. A workplace is a structured place where you perform certain duties in return for a wage. It can be public, private, or even your enterprise. The common feature of these workplaces is that they are all structured and mostly embrace work methods, regulations, procedures, and written or adopted cultures to follow to induce order to achieve the aspired goals.

Workplaces are generally called establishments, which are categorized into institutions, corporations, companies, firms, and so on. Government-related functions are as old as the history of man, but early versions surely did not have today's modern structure and organization. For the private sector, the history of man does not record any company, firm, corporation, or institution in the form that exists today. The oldest company that came into existence was United Dutch Chartered East Indian, which was established in 1602 to manage the trading part of the Dutch colonies. Before that, in 1472, the first bank, Banca Monte Di Siena, was established in Italy for giving loans to sailors and traders as advanced cash earnings on bank interest. In 1666, the British government established the first insurance company immediately after the great London fire to insure properties and goods, which later extended to insuring trading ships.

Man's experience in managing structured, organized, and prescribed work environments amounts to no longer than five hundred years in the recorded history of twelve thousand years. This experience is short and thin compared to man's experience in science, medicine, agriculture, sailing, literature, and philosophy, which is immense and extensive. These first establishments were mostly started by military personnel as part of colonial establishments, with a military management style. Possibly, that was suitable for the work environments with limited skills and calibers available then.

THE BIRTH OF MODERN MANAGEMENT

The modern management of people and work was first initiated in the early twentieth century by Henry Fayol, a French mining engineer, mining executive, author, and director of mines, who was known as the founder of modern management theory. He developed fourteen principles of management that act as a guide for managers to perform managerial activities. He also created a general theory of business administration that is often called Fayolism. Fayol's work was well received by Frederick Taylor, an American mechanical engineer who was widely known for his methods of improving industrial efficiency. Taylor was one of the first management consultants. In 1909, Taylor published his efficiency techniques in his book *The Principles of Scientific Management*, which the Academy of Management voted as the most influential management book in 2001.

Fayol and Taylor were the first to introduce organizational behavior with limited impact on the behavior of the workers as individuals and as groups. The work management remained vastly based on the military management style for a long time. Both Fayol and Taylor focused on the methods of work, rather than on developing human skills and behavior. Every attempt in this direction was to serve the production lines and increase production volumes.

The human factor in the place of work was neglected for a long time, highly exploited, unjustly compensated, and badly treated, until the 1940s and '50s, when workers started calling for better working conditions, amenities, and rights. This movement urged governments

cause massive waste and damage on all sides. In societies, it can create civil havoc.

Most corporations focus more on material than nonmaterial incentives. Although there is no one rule for all, it is more effective to categorize people and customize their incentives. Money, as an incentive, is always welcome by all but has repercussion power. At the time of dispersion of incentives, bonuses, or end-of-the-year pay rises, most people get a jubilant feeling only until they start comparing theirs with others' generally and with peers' of similar rankings specifically. Traditionally, incentives, bonuses, and pay raises are dispersed at the beginning of the year, but some have fiscal years beginning on other dates. For many, that means a worse time to gauge the levels of employee satisfaction. The sense of differential is more powerful than the monetary amount. That is, a sense of justice is more important than material gain. The first is intrinsic, and the second is extrinsic. You may go on to disperse more money in this way, only to upset people more. Maybe this is what you think is right to do to make people more motivated, as we all are short of experience in this field. Or it is done on purpose by emotionally dispositioned executives and leaders as a cynical, Machiavellian approach with the urge of putting everyone under their narcissist desires.

Abraham Maslow was an American psychologist who created Maslow's hierarchy of needs, which is also known as Maslow's pyramid of needs, a theory of psychological health predicated on fulfilling innate human needs in priority, culminating in self-actualization. Maslow devised the pyramid in 1943. It was one of the most cognitive ideas in behavioral science and was the first to introduce a humanistic approach to the management of people at work. He basically said that human needs are at five stages, starting with physiological needs, followed by safety and security, love and belongingness, self-esteem, and, finally, self-actualization. Maslow's more important finding was that these five stages must be satisfied in ascending order, and no stage can be jumped over. Said another way, a need cannot be satisfied until the preceding need is satisfied.

In many corporations and societies, the approach to meeting a need is jumbled, not achieving the desired objectives. These corporations and societies focus more and more on the basic physiological needs, which are extrinsic, leaving higher needs, which are intrinsic, unattended to or marginally entertained. The pyramid of needs gets inflated and overly reinforced at the base, only to hold featherweights along the top. This is one approach that narcissistic superiors use to abuse staff.

MACHIAVELLIAN NARCISSIST EXECUTIVES AND LEADERS

Machiavellian narcissist executives and leaders are unconsciously effective in disrupting the order of the needs, creating chaos in the place of work and society.

No one can win with narcissist executives and leaders if they have the power in hand, and no one should expect them to come to their senses. They may come under pressure of their superiors or the force of law to behave themselves, but that is like holding a ball underwater and claiming there is no ball. The ball will pop up when even the slightest opportunity arises. These executives and leaders, at the highest levels of narcissism, are bound to eventually destroy themselves and their surroundings.

Narcissistic people do not appear only at places of work or in political arenas; they also appear in families, in social clubs, among friends, and in religious groups. I have also seen some among spiritual teachers. We are all on the scale of narcissism, with varying degrees. On a scale of ten, up to four is not serious, but it is still a behavioral defect. At the top come dictatorial individuals, managers, social and political players, parents, elder siblings, business leaders, and countless others, who share the common feature of being a menace to others. Narcissistic individuals are bound to be irrational. We are all irrational to varying degrees, as mentioned earlier.

It is impossible to change other people, because they have their own set of layers of memories, which respond to millions of variables, both external and internal triggers in vastly different forms and configurations. You also cannot avoid them all for a long time. Your rescue lies in your awareness of the reality of life and raising the level of your consciousness to bring a reasonably practical level of harmony into your behavior and reflect it on others.

Numerous sources help individuals to build skills to observe and gauge the character of fellow humans and see into their own deep-rooted traits. We all need to work on two fronts with different dynamics. One is to return home to our origin to actualize our suppressed higher selves. The second is to revoke the worst that other people can inflict on us.

THE ULTIMATE ASPIRATION

Our ultimate aspiration in life is to live to our full self-actualization with purpose and realistic contentment and to depart peacefully. This aspiration would have been easily attainable had you been born as another creature in this world, like an animal. To the extent we are aware, animals have only physical needs. Even the cruelest animals, once they are fully fed, are astonishingly peaceful, safe, and even playful. This is a mere survival issue for animals that life begins and ends with. Animals do not have processing and judgmental minds. The animal mind is merely a functional mind, which is fully programmed and on autopilot mode. By implication, animals do not have an ego.

For human beings, life begins with a physical need. Today our physical needs are well placed and conveniently accessed. Items are readily available and attainable like never before in the history of humanity. Items that the wealthiest people could not afford to buy are now comfortably enjoyed by people with ordinary incomes. With human beings, the problems start here: when the basic needs are satisfied, the psychological needs, most of which are egoic needs, start bursting in all directions. Hungry people, like animals, are always busy looking for food and have no time to create problems. Problems are created by people who have full stomachs.

CHAPTER 5

MIND AND ENERGY

THE MIND

THIS LIFE CONDITION REVEALS THE fact that a human being is made up of more than the body. The mind of a human being is another critical component. It is the central processing unit. It is meant to process commands consciously given by the mind holder. That is the conscious use of the mind that human beings have used to generate fabulous ideas, inventions, solutions, remedies, and numerous facilities that have improved human life to a great extent. This mind now has another user who can only misuse and abuse it for fictitious and malicious purposes.

IT IS THE EGO

The rightful user of the mind—that is, the mind holder—cannot fully use the mind, because the ego is constantly interfering and disturbing the healthy conscious processing of thoughts. The ego play is now almost a permanent feature of the human mind, affecting the course of life in a disturbing manner. The intensity of the disturbance differs among people. But a fact remains common among all: what happens in the mind affects what happens in the body and vice versa. Every incident in your mind creates a fluctuation in the level of the mind, which has a chemical reaction, and in turn, every chemical reaction generates a fluctuation in the level of mind, which is a dollop effect. The mind is not just the brain, and it is not located in the head only, as a single human anatomy. Instead, every single one of the hundred trillion cells in your entire body has its own intelligence. Your mind is in your entire body. Your body is the hardware that embodies the software and storage capacity.

Your body-mind hardware and software, like your computer, need energy to function.

ENERGY

The third component of human formation is energy.

If you keep your body energy in perfect balance, it flows universally over your body in a cyclic loop and keeps the voltage in each cell at 1.4 volts. A proper diet is an essential part of energy stability. Body stretching, long walks, massages, and other exercises help to unblock any parts of your body that hinder the flow of energy. These could be muscle cramps, joint dislocation, intestinal twists, chronic headaches, and, most importantly, the misalignment of the spine. It is purported that if you keep your energy component in perfect balance, there will be no disease in your physical and mental components. Even hereditary or genetic diseases are not absolute and can be avoided or cured. If you keep the cells' voltage at 1.4, the immune system will function against all diseases. Bringing harmony and vitality to the flow of energy in the body will alienate diseases. There are numerous reported cases of malignant diseases that have been cured by meditation and intense energy focus.

These three dimensions of the self—body, mind, and energy—are essentially physical in nature and can be sensed by our five sense organs. Each is more delicate than the preceding one.

ETHER

The fourth component is ether. It is beyond our sense of perception. It is neither physical nor nonphysical. We cannot experience it in a normal environment, as the five senses cannot perceive it. You can, however, access this layer of your dimension if you can shut down your five senses. If you reach this layer, you access cosmic knowledge that is beyond explanation. Some ancient thinkers and ascetics could reach this source and receive the intended knowledge. None of them could explain the scientific rationale behind their findings. The findings were simply downloaded. The ancient Romans were the first to discover the solar system some three thousand years ago, and the first telescope was invented only four hundred years ago. Numerous scientific discoveries were made by Muslim scientists over the past 1,400 years in the areas of cosmology, astrology, astronomy, medicine, and more, when no such facilities were available to support researchers and developers, as in the present time. For example, Muhammad al-Khwarizmi introduced the algorithm that operates as the basis of space missions and artificial intelligence (AI). His intricate data spreads today require a giant computer to process, analyze, and build models. How did he arrive at the applicability of his findings, which surely were and are profoundly applicable? Most researchers, developers, authors, and reformers confess that many of their findings are supported by facilities, laboratory apparatuses, computer-aided simulators, peer critiques, and more, but somewhere along their work, something more like a sensation pops up and gives the information, the idea, or the answer—a eureka moment of euphoria. *Eureka* means "I have found it" in the Greek language. Greek mathematician and physician Archimedes shouted it when he discovered the method of measuring the volume of irregular shapes. Archimedes did not say, "I invented," "I developed," or "I created"; he simply said, "I found it," implying "It was there, and I received it."

These seekers usually get near the etheric layer, somehow face a slit in the path of the cosmos at a time when they have exhausted the five senses and reached full despondency and emptiness, and then receive the answer.

Helen Schucman did not like to be mentioned as the author of the book titled *A Course in Miracles*. The book is voluminous, profoundly enlightening, and astonishingly applicable. Helen worked with William Thetford in the College of Physicians and Surgeons at Columbia University. In the summer of 1965, after years of conflict between

William and Helen and within their department, William, in an impassioned talk with Helen, said, "There must be another way"—a way people could cooperate rather than compete. Helen agreed to join William to seek solutions.

Soon after, Helen started having a series of inner visions, which culminated in the fall of 1965, when she heard an inner voice say to her, "This is a course in miracles. Please take notes." The same voice then loaded the course onto her. Helen spent seven years scribing the book in shorthand and later dictated it to William, who typed it up. Helen did not have the knowledge and skills of the content of the book prior to the incident of scribing it. The information was not in the memories of Helen and not in her archives or bookshelves, which is why she and William suffered the lack of it. We know now how she received it: from the etheric zone.

Sadguru, in his book *Inner Engineering*, mentions that in partnership with a friend, he became a successful businessman in the construction industry. He says when whatever you do is a success, suddenly, you start believing that the planets revolve around you, not the sun. That is the kind of young man he was until one fateful afternoon in September 1982, when he decided to get on his motorcycle and ride up Chamundi Hill in India. He had no clue his life would never be the same again. He became a man with tremendous, ecstatic energy, a glorified and venerable presence. Wherever he went, people asked him for his blessings. Sadguru was transformed and transcended but never mentioned what had happened up on Chamundi Hill and how. He entered the etheric zone. The majority of those who touch or enter this zone do not want to reveal certain information, as in near-death cases. To a point, they ask you to stop asking. In one case, a Palestinian member of the government, Saeb Erekat, in a TV interview, just said what others who'd had near-death experiences had said before. They all say the same things but stop at a point. When Saeb Erekat was pushed by the interviewer to explain more, he told her bluntly not to go any further. The only useful answer she got out of him came when she asked if it was a pleasant journey. He replied, "Look at my smile!" He died two months later, in November 2022.

Eckhart Tolle, in his first and most well-received book, *The Power of*

Now, mentioned that one night not long after his twenty-ninth birthday, after having lived in a state of almost continuous anxiety interspersed with periods of suicidal depression, he woke up in the early hours with a feeling of absolute dread. It was not the first time he had woken up in that state, but this time, the feeling was more intense than it had ever been. It created in him a deep loathing of the world and, worse, loathing of his existence in the world. He wondered what the point was in continuing to live. His feeling grew for annihilation. He kept repeating to himself, "I cannot live with myself any longer." Then, suddenly, he became aware of the thought *Am I one or two?*

He asked himself, and then he became aware of the duality in himself, *I* and *self*, and realized only one of them is real. He was stunned by the realization that his mind stopped, and he became fully conscious. Then he was drawn into what seemed like a vortex of energy and was gripped by intense fear, when he heard the words "Resist nothing."

Suddenly, there was no more fear, and he felt himself fall into a void, after which, he says, he has no recollection. After that incident, Tolle's life changed, becoming more serene and pleasant, forever. Tolle has been one of the most successful spiritual teachers in the world. He had to go to that despondency tipping point to shut down his five senses to reach the etheric border and fall into it. His narrative resembles the experiences mentioned earlier.

There are common features of the experiences of those who have reached the etheric layer: reaching the despondency point, shutting down the five senses, touching the etheric border, falling into it to receive information that is mostly private, dropping all baggage of the world, and living ecstatically ever after.

It is widely acknowledged that reaching the etheric is possible but requires intense focus and endured stillness for extended periods, which may not be practical for many people.

ALIGNING THE LAYERS

Our role is to align the first three layers: the body, mind, and energy. Simple conscious breathing, sense perception, long walks, body stretching, body massage, and frequent short stillness retreats are all we need at the practical level to align our body, mind, and energy layers.

The ultimate reach is to understand our physical and nonphysical dynamics to enable ourselves to understand others for more harmonious encounters and well-being. In any direction we take, it is paramount to understand that others are exactly like us, and we only differ in narratives. The better ones are of higher consciousness—no more and no less. When we describe people's behavior as the second person, it must be understood that includes us. This will prevent us from pointing and blaming or accusing others for our undesired conditions.

CHAPTER 6

WHO IS WHAT?: PERSONALITY TRAITS

CONSCIOUS OR UNCONSCIOUS

H UMAN BEINGS ARE EITHER CONSCIOUS or unconscious, and in between the two are tens of degrees of intensities. These degrees of intensities translate into varying facets and functions of human behavior. I have not known anyone who is fully conscious. I know a few who are deeply unconscious. These are either historical, known for their atrocities, or living, known for their potential to create upheavals. Just watch the news, and you will pick up a few; and if you look around at work and in society, you will find you are not short of them.

Unconsciousness is a state of the mind; it is not a behavioral tendency. It is a gateway for inducing various behavioral traits. Narcissistic behavior is the major trait that proliferates in all of us. By implication, narcissists are unconscious; their minds dwell in either the past or the future, both of which are unreal, which leads to irrational manners. Therefore, to this point, we are all unconscious, narcissistic, and irrational in varying intensities. The intensity of our fouls is a critical factor that makes us different, and to some extent, we accept them as social realities. We are on the same boat, but some are less bothering or more bothering than others.

On a scale of ten, the most intense narcissistic type sits at the top. A person all the way down to four is considered an agitating narcissistic.

Below four, the narcissistic type is manageable and, to a limit, can be transformed into an added value, as the energies at this level are more docile, agile, and attainable. However, we should be vigilant about how to stay watchful of all degrees of narcissistic people and strive to induce consciousness in self and others as the ultimate aspiration of humanity.

INTENSE NARCISSISTS

Narcissists come in many intensities and shapes, but they all share the same behaviors and bitterness. When we understand the intense narcissist, we will be able to understand the rest. Any type of narcissist who comes below the intense narcissist is a mere reduced version of it. The intensity of our narcissism is developed based on our life experience, including our genetic formation.

The moment we are born is the moment we are in our complete form and self and have all the knowledge it takes to live in this world; that is divine knowledge, as explained earlier, which conforms with most religious and spiritual teachings. To reiterate, Indian Brahma Kumaris spiritual teachings specify these needs as happiness, love, peace, knowledge, wisdom, purity, and power.

At this moment, we are self-sufficient except for physical endurance and needs, which we take a few years to acquire. Some animals can naturally become self-dependent in a few minutes, while others take a few hours or days.

A few hours after our birth, we are given a name, nationality, religion, or caste. In some societies, they even decide our future spouse. We are unaware of these at the time but probably are going to defend and fight for them later in life. After our birth, the parents and caretakers are supposed to feed us, wash us, protect us against dangers, and keep us healthy. Our other needs are already embodied in us by the divine. For this reason, parents and caretakers are not supposed to intervene or interfere with us as children during our upbringing and influence our thoughts and emotions. Firstly, we have what we need in this life. Secondly, what the parents and caretakers have and want to give us Is already contaminated by their experiences. It is more sensible that they learn from the children than teach them. Any attempt to influence the children, probably with goodwill, is going to induce all sorts of memories in them that range from overprotection to abandonment, both of which shrink the inner self of children and lower their consciousness, inducing narcissism in them for the rest of their lives. This is the point in time when human beings detour from the natural path of life.

Kahlil Gibran, a Lebanese American, in his famous book *The Prophet*, says the following in prose:

> Your children are not your children.
> `They are sons and daughters of Life longing for itself.
> They come through you but not from you.
> And though they are with you, they belong not to you.
> You may give them your love* but not your thoughts.
> For they have their thoughts.
> You may house their bodies but not their souls.
> For their souls dwell in the house of tomorrow, which you cannot visit, not even in your dreams.
> You may strive to be like them but seek not to make them like you.
> For life goes not backward nor tarries with yesterday.

If we would let children grow naturally, as Gibran implies, many of the childhood egoic memories would not form, and probably, the adolescence and adulthood egoic memories would be filtered to their tiniest information.

THE LOVING, INNOCENT ENEMY

The mother is the first person to tamper with your divine inner self's stability and balance. She does to you what she thinks is good for you. But what she thinks is good for you and what is right for you are vastly apart. What she does for you stems from what she has and what she is herself. As with most people in the world, her attitude, personality, and behavior are highly contaminated by her genetic limitations and

---

* *Love* means *kindness* in the Arabic version.

41

the incalculable life situations she encountered during her childhood, adolescence, and adulthood, which were absorbed through her egoic thoughts and reactions. Now she is dumping them in you, in good faith, drawing you into an unconscious state, which eventually converts you into a narcissist. The intensity of your narcissism is a worse replica of your mother. The best or the worst of your mother, unfortunately, produces the same result. An overly caring, protective, and loving mother and a cold, abusive, and abandoning mother both prevent you from reaching and realizing your inner self and convert you into a narcissist, which puts you in a state of unconsciousness, in which you want to mask your behavior to portray a personality that suits the surroundings and your hidden intentions. These personalities include active narcissists, passive narcissists, extrovert narcissists, and introvert narcissists. These behavioral traits normally come not in single traits but in complex combinations of two or more, which make your behavior profoundly sophisticated and hard to understand and deal with in normal life situations.

NARCISSIST BEHAVIORS

These combinations in their crude forms include the

- active extrovert narcissist,
- passive extrovert narcissist,
- active introvert narcissist, and
- passive introvert narcissist.

The best way to understand the behavior of each combination is to separate the components and learn their tendencies individually. The common factor among all combinations is that all are narcissists, which means, as mentioned earlier, they are all unconscious in varying intensities, culminating in intense narcissists. Therefore, all narcissists have a disability in seeing reality as it is. Instead, they see and interpret life situations according to what their interpreters offer them, based on the memory processes. The interpreter is the ego, which always offers an illusionary perception that agitates wrong or exaggerated emotions and eventual external or internal reactions. The tendency of each narcissistic trait is separately illustrated.

1. Active narcissists actively distort reality. They have imposing manners, forcing their narcissistic needs both physically by aggressive postures or forces and verbally by falsifying, betraying, and lying. This personality profile is a nuisance and harmful to others.

2. Extrovert narcissists need to attract attention constantly to satisfy their ego, stay vibrant, and catch the eye. They exhibit larger-than-life self-images and grandiosity. They become cumbersome, hard to swallow, and pathetic. They need many friends, particularly of the opposite gender, and like to change them frequently to have fresh attentions that never end.

    This personality profile is outwardly confident and looks strong and brave, only to conceal the opposites hidden in the inner self. This personality profile is proactively devious.

    Combine the three profiles of active extrovert narcissists and see what an upheaval you have to endure should you have this person around you or, even worse, above you.

3. Passive narcissists are more prone to avoid reality by hiding it than to show the false self and stay more in a reserved and withdrawn mode. They look for shortfalls and inferior qualities in others to feed their egos. They are skillful in spreading rumors and creating discord among others.

    Create another combination of passive extrovert narcissist, and see how much your life at work or in society is stretched, your career and social life are paralyzed, and your health is continuously threatened.

4. Introvert narcissists live lives full of fantasies and fall deep into them. They tend to use people against one another by creating proxy rivalries, intentionally pushing people away to increase their unworthiness. They are skillful in creating pseudo–life situations for people, increasing their risks and danger zones.

    Create the fourth combination of passive introvert narcissist, and you will have a recipe for depressive anxiety that will run into your major body organs, alienating your health and well-being to dire proportions.

The borderlines between the profiles are permeable; they overlap and produce confusing behaviors in individuals, adding more to their behavioral displacement. As defective as they are, they serve the purpose of hunters, who are equally or more defective in their own behaviors. Hunters come in different masks and attire and have needs that can be satisfied by the defective behaviors of others.

HUNTER RECRUITER

John Perkins, American author of the book titled *Confessions of an Economic Hit Man*, explains in chapter 1 that he was recruited by the National Security Agency (NSA), the largest spy organization in the USA, for all the defective attributes he had. Knowing his own profile, he assumed he would be rejected. The recruitment assessment had little to do with the positive issues he did not have. The negative issues, such as the frustrations in his life, his anger at his parents, an obsession with women, and his ambition to live the good life, gave the recruiter a hook. In addition, Perkins explains, he was seducible and rebellious against his father, and he'd shown his willingness to lie to the police in an incident in which his friend Farhad was in trouble. Perkins confirmed these types of attributes were exactly what the agency sought, and from NSA's viewpoint, these negatives were positive. A few weeks after NSA testing, Perkins was offered a job to start training in the art of spying.

ENMESHED OR ABANDONED

These four behavioral profiles you may have lived with or come across in various places, starting from your mother, father, siblings, and family members and other people in society, at work, and elsewhere. All these people have affected your behavior in many ways, means, and intensities. Also, you've affected their behavior in similar manners. But your childhood period was the most impactful period, and your mother and then your father had the most potent thrust on your inner self and consequent behavior for rest of your life. Your parents handled you in one of two ways: enmeshed or abandoned, in between which exists a spectrum of varying degrees of intensities. Both types of handling produce the same impact on the child: shrinking and restricting the child's inner self. Most cases that have been reported are related to abandoned, rather than enmeshed, children. Both have created astonishing successes and tragedies.

EARNED OR INHERITED SUCCESS

We can look at the biographies of many renowned personalities who produced exceptional products of human talents or committed acts out of human imagination and expectation from these two categories at heavy ends. Some of these personalities include Joseph Stalin, Fyodor Dostoyevsky, Leo Tolstoy, Anton Chekhov, Gabrielle "Coco" Chanel, and Buddha, who was tightly enmeshed in a royalty cage for thirty-two years of his life, along with many more. These famed people had abnormal childhoods in various ways, but all of them were injured psychologically, emotionally, and/or physically. These were negative experiences that produced energies that could not be expressed or externally utilized for various reasons, such as hypnotic conditions of young children or fear by older children. Instead, they were repressed, rebounded, and stored in the related memory cells. Rebounded stored memory is called *pain body* by Eckhart Tolle. Whatever the cause of their generation, they remain as energies. Like information, they are neutral until they are used. They can be used for good purposes or bad purposes and made positive or negative. The ego, which occupies the minds of most people most of the time, converts the pain body into negative thoughts and emotions and, inevitably, negative reactions that produce more adversities and pains that are counterproductive to freeing the inner self and connecting to the divine source of self-realization.

On the other hand, the energies of the pain body can be converted into positive emotions and produce useful results. These energies appear naturally under harsh conditions when people face imminent dangers or reach a level of full despondency that requires them to make a decision or take action.

At the age of around ten, in primary school, I ran away from an imminent danger only to face a high boundary wall that was too high for my height then. I had two choices: face the schoolboys' mob, which was out of the question, or jump over the boundary wall, which did not appear possible. I decided to jump with all my will and survival needs, so I did. Until today, I cannot figure out what energy pushed me up over the boundary wall. The fact remains that the energy did the work, but where did it come from? Undoubtedly, it came from within me, not from any external source. It was my rebounded and repressed energy, my pain body.

There are people in the world who inherited success, wealth, fame, and popularity without actually earning them. But those who succeeded on merit were blessed by the pain of life situations, when they found nothing more to lose and started gaining by opening up to the opportunities. When opportunities arrive, you must have enough deferred energies to handle them. The most disadvantaged children have the most deferred energies, which are manifested in their life journeys' later achievements and success. These people naturally earn a sense of grandeur, which is real and solid, while others are bound to be sabotaged by their ego-induced sense of grandiosity, which is imaginary and self-defeating.

THE CHIEF EXECUTIVE OFFICER

One time, I was invited to a gala dinner to listen to a speech by the chief executive officer of a large company in my country, Bahrain, who was asked to share his success story. Listening to his talk, I gathered he was a successful person and CEO. What caught my attention was his realistic view of his success. He mentioned that his initial job in the company had been purchasing officer. He'd climbed to a senior position in the same department, and then many changes had happened in the company's organizational structure; many of the older executives had been removed, which had made way for him to climb the ladder further up. After a relatively short time, redundancy of more highly paid executives had occurred, which had led the way for him to reach the second layer of the organization. Two years later, the former chief executive officer had resigned, nominating him for his replacement. At the end of his speech, he declared naturally and humbly that had those changes not happened, he would have still been working as the purchasing officer. His fast promotions did not delude him but made him invest in the opportunities' merit fully.

Another success story was told by another CEO of a financial organization. Although he earned the position rightfully, he singled himself out by crediting all his achievements to himself, when opportunities around him at the time were like no other time before or after. The first success story will lead the person to contentment and further consciousness, and unfortunately, the second one is heading toward yearning for more recognition and attention that will never end, which may lead him to depression and restlessness unless bliss is bestowed upon him.

Swiss psychiatrist and psychoanalyst Carl Jung, who pioneered analytical psychology, said that man is less good than he imagines himself or wants to be.

CHAPTER 7

SALVATION AND HUMAN MADNESS

LOW CONSCIOUSNESS

IT IS MORE EVIDENT THAN not that life will not change at a conscious level to any sizeable degree in the foreseeable future or, probably, in our lifetime. A hypothetical measure suggests that if full human salvation, implying full consciousness and presence, is at the score of ten on a scale of ten, the present score is 2.27. This suggests our consciousness, at individual and collective levels, has not reached even one-third of salvation. It has taken us at least about eighy thousand years to reach this level, which makes us just conscious enough not to physically bump into one another or street light posts or run into one another's cars. We need to be highly vigilant in this world, as we are just awake and not conscious enough to secure even an encouraging level of well-being. We need to continue our quest for more and better awareness of our behavioral dysfunctions, attempting to induce more consciousness and honor our purpose in this world.

Your four layers of memories—genetic, childhood, adolescence, and adulthood—make up your attitude, and your attitude shapes your personality, which in turn exposes your behaviors. Narcissistic behavior, with all its facets, is one common behavior that agitates life everywhere all the time and is maddening to destructive limits. We all are contributors to this effect.

Pioneering English physicist, mathematician, and theologian Sir Isaac Newton said, "I can calculate the motion of heavenly bodies but cannot the madness of people." Similarly, Albert Einstein, German American developer of the theory of relativity, said, "Only two things are infinite, the universe and human stupidity, but I'm not sure about the former." Jesus (PBUH)** once said to his cult, "I managed to resurrect the dead but could not correct your minds." Ramana Maharshi, a great Indian spiritual guru, said in his teachings, "The mind is ill." Buddha said the human mind normally generates suffering, dissatisfaction, and misery. The book of Islam, the Koran, repeatedly reminds us that most people are immoral, ignorant, and senseless, and numerous verses reflect negative features stemming from the human mind. Tolle states that if the history of humanity were the clinical case history of a single human being, the diagnosis would have to be chronic paranoid delusion, with a pathological propensity to commit murder and acts of extreme violence against his perceived enemies.

The essence of human history constitutes human savageness and madness. If we think things have changed, we are adding more madness to life.

We can now imagine the intensity and heaviness of our misfits that we are carrying on our shoulders and the duties that are bestowed on humanity to flower hopes in the minds and hearts of billions of people.

The first step in this direction is to recognize one's insanity, which itself is the emergence of sanity.

WHAT YOU ARE NOT IS WHAT YOU ARE

Hitherto, you have been going through the delusionary life that humanity has been going through, mostly creating false sceneries leading to agonies and detouring the divine purpose of life. Most of what you have been following in this reading is introducing you to what you are not, or at least what you should not be. When you find what you are not, what you are will stand out naturally.

** Peach be upon him.

49

NOT DOING IS AWARENESS

In the industrial engineering field, which was my initial job, the main target was always to increase the efficiency and quality of the products and services. We used scientific techniques to map the processes involved in producing products or services. Then we focused on studying better ways to perform the processes. In almost all cases, we improved the methods and increased production or service levels. The whole initiative was about doing things faster. In doing things faster, we produced more of the output, but we discovered the increased output was not met with increased sales and earnings. So what was the point of speeding up the processes? We found out that in many cases, there were numerous processes undertaken, including those improved, that did not contribute value to the end products or services; we called them non-value-added activities. Using another technique, we traced these non-value-added activities and mostly managed to eliminate or reduce them. With this intervention, the cost came down; products and services were offered and sold at lower prices, which led to increased sales and profit levels.

There were cases in which the end output was not needed at all, but tremendous efforts were put in to produce more of what was not needed by intelligent interventions. One example is the cleaning of a train station's platforms and walkways. Intelligent intervention took place, looking at high-tech tools and equipment, and achieved the objective of cleaning well and fast but increased the cost. An unintelligent idea came through from a young outsider posing a seemingly stupid question: "Why do you have to clean the platforms? If you don't make them dirty, you don't need to clean them." The focus shifted from what to do to what not to do. Hygiene regulations and procedures were put in place that required everyone on the platform not to make the place dirty, which served the purpose and also reduced the running cost.

The field of industrial engineering always targets the non-value-added activities. We have empirically established that 72 percent of activities are non-value-added activities, and 20 percent are value-added activities that are not performed efficiently and require improvement. Only 8 percent of activities are performed at the precision level.

After completion of each project in this field, an assessment is drawn to establish the lessons learned to apply to future projects. Lessons accumulated over the years indicated that the majority—80 percent—of firms focus on the efficiency of activities, in isolation of the effectiveness. This is embarking on the improvement work before questioning if the activity is necessary at all in the first place. It is producing what is unnecessary or wasteful more efficiently and in better ways or committing production flaws and then striving to improve on the method of committing them. The root cause is the management in these firms; with long service periods and experience, they are unaware of such dysfunctions of work processes and are hooked on past invalid practices. Most findings revealed that practices were long established and taken over by successors who continued without questioning them; moreover, most people around workplaces are deeply entrenched in these work practices that require enlightening, replacing, or updating. The management and workers in these firms are highly disciplined to perform the old versions of the practices, which are irrelevant to their true present realities. The workplace has turned into a temple full of ancient dogmatic work practices performed like rituals with devotion. Here too the ego is at work, incessantly holding people in the past and being fed progressively unconsciously, pulling the work methods to stagnation, inertia, and then termination. This is how unconsciousness leads to company failure and closure.

Anywhere in the world is like the place of work. We behave and perform not according to our true selves (conscious selves) but according to our false selves (unconscious selves). If we find what we should not do as false selves, what we should do as true selves will stand out naturally.

SALVATION AND SAVIOR

Tolle, in his second book, *A New Earth*, disseminates a great deal of hope for a better earth for all. This hope is shared by many religions, spiritual traditions, philosophers, and scientists who also share a common insight that our normal state of mind is heavily burdened by clogged dysfunctions of egoic thoughts. The hope, real and ponderous, blends aspiration with the responsibility that someday, on the high horizon, the transformation of human consciousness will arise. This transformation has been mentioned in all known religions and spiritual teachings, with words like *the straight path, enlightenment, salvation, the end of suffering, liberation, awakening,* and many other terms. Some teachings offer two passages for transformation: the passage of a straight or true path inward to the true self and the passage of detour path that is away from the false self. Each requires different force, focus, and endurance but creates the same transformation of human consciousness. In many religions and spiritual teachings, there is a mention of the arrival or resurrection of a savior who will bestow peace, serenity, tranquility, and justice on all people. Some books describe the arrival of a savior and claim transformation of human life will take place as a sudden event; others expect it as a process that will take a long period, as was the case with the prophets of the major religions, who came gradually and spent many years delivering their messages. The big-bang approach never happened in the history of mankind, except for natural disasters and uproars that lead to the wiping of human congregations and reformed living conditions. In Brahma Kumaris teaching, it is believed we are now in a confluence age, going into a golden age (meaning a transformation age) that necessitates a disastrous force to enter, hence the expectation of major upheavals in the coming times.

All these teachings and speculations suggest a better, not worse, earth for all. That is the same as for any sudden enlightenment stemming from a despondency position, called *sotar* in India. The narration of these prognoses is highly metaphoric and requires jurisprudence and some scientific substantiations.

The good news is that we all, from all cultures and religions, are hopeful that better times are ahead of us, but we need to endure some more hardship.

WISE APPROACH

The wisest approach to realizing a transformation of human consciousness's hopes is to take part in it on an individual level, and the first step is to know what you are by knowing what you are not. As Tolle says, recognizing one's own insanity is the arising of sanity.

What you are not is what your thoughts tell you that you are or what you want to be. These thoughts are agitated by the ego, based on the triggers it receives from your five senses. Then, by tapping into the four layers of your memories, it formulates thought packages that suit its mischievous missions and delivers them in your mind, convincing you they are your thoughts based on your life circumstances and are real. Almost always, the thoughts you receive are negative, agitating, agonizing, and debilitating. Never in your life should you expect anything favorable from your thoughts. These thoughts will generate corresponding feelings, mostly of anger, fear, grudge, restlessness, anguish, jealousy, vengeance, and so on. These feelings will push you toward verbal and physical actions toward others or yourself by rebounding them. You might even hurt yourself physically. These actions will portray your behavior. If the same behavior is repeated in an incessant manner, it solidifies and forms your attitude, which will be sent back to your memory storage to await future calls that will operate another round trip of thoughts, emotions, actions, and behavior. This makes up your personality that people call you for, which is your egoic personality, your false personality. This personality travels with you all the time. Depending on its intensity, it overturns your perception of reality and your true self and increases your level of unconsciousness. As a reflection, you become disconnected from reality, which makes you narcissistic, irrational, or mad, depending on its intensity. At this stage, all these emotions take place inside you, in your privacy. In these conditions, you are prone to all sorts of attractions or repulsions that are malicious to you, which will eventually lead you to repeat mistakes, inflicting harm on others and yourself. You might develop addictions to things, alcohol, drugs, sex, and compulsive eating.

When you meet others, depending on the level of their unconsciousness, which is their level of narcissism or madness, your interactions with them will be anything but peaceful or healthy. You will, however, restrain your behavior by repressing your feelings and emotions, conforming to certain traditions and regulations, and protecting yourself against accidents or dangers. You are usually able to practice restraint for a while, but the moment you are over with, your behavior will revert. During the period of your restraint, all your thoughts are there; your mind is clogged, as usual; and you are not aware of it, so you do not push your ego away, and no space is created in your mind. That's why you feel overly exhausted and then, after you finish your play of restraint, feel relieved. That restraint is good for the place you are in and for your safety but is unhealthy for your emotional state, your nervous system, and your physical health. If the restraint is repeated in this manner, it will undoubtedly inflict on you multiple malignant diseases. The better approach is to become aware and present in situations that require certain types of behaviors. Awareness and presence will give all the wisdom you require in any situation without your withholding emotions or acting unduly.

YOUR MIND DECIDES YOUR HEALTH

Your physical and mental health is highly affected by what dwells in your mind, which also affects your surroundings and the place you are in. This could be your home, your workplace, or even a place you just enter for a short visit.

Masaru Emoto, a Japanese researcher, experimented on water samples from the same source. He had each sample in a small glass container. Then he picked up a sample, recited positive talk on it, and placed it in a freezer to turn it into ice. The same process he repeated with another sample, but this time, he recited negative talk on it. Both samples were then put under a microscope for observation. The sample with positive words showed the ice crystals in clear geometric shapes. The sample with negative words showed dim, murky, uneven shapes. Moto repeated this experiment on both types ten thousand times. He found the same basic results but also discovered that using different positive and negative words each time produced different shapes and clarity in the ice samples such that each word produced its own effect on the ice. Unfortunately, Emoto could not substantiate his findings with empirical and scientific shreds of evidence. Finally, in the year 2017, an insightful and astonishing book was published by the Institute of Stuttgart, titled *Water and Its Memory*, which provided evidence of the fact that water is profoundly receptive and susceptive to the types and quality of words and thoughts it receives. Moreover, another experiment was conducted in Iran in 2022 in a similar manner, but the specimens were two half apples. Each half was placed and covered in a separate container. This time, positive words were written on one container, negative words were written on the other container, and the containers were left for ten hours. The result showed the half apple with positive writing had normal deformation and shrinkage, while the other one was decomposed and rotten.

Our body is made up of 70 percent water, and the rest is processed food, both of which have been proven to produce reactions, delicately and swiftly, to the words they are exposed to. The words are thoughts that do not even need to be voiced.

We all have experienced people with positive thoughts enter a room and disseminate positive vibes that give others a sense of comfort and serenity, while one with negative thoughts sucks your energy and irritates you. This happens without either of them even saying a word.

CHAPTER 8

ONLY ONE PROBLEM AND
ONLY ONE SOLUTION

AWARENESS OF SELF AND OTHERS

THE WORK OF TOLLE, WITH respect to consciousness, is profoundly practical and effective. In his writings and his talks, you can gather that there is always one problem in the world, and there is always one solution for it. The problem is that people are mostly unconscious, and the solution is to elevate their consciousness. Awareness of this fact is a major step in relieving humanity of its heavy and destructive burden.

Awareness of self and of others' behavior, as already mentioned, is the wisest path to follow. When you elevate your level of consciousness, every other attempt becomes easier. You will understand the behaviors of other people with great clarity, and your empathy will strengthen. You will, drop by drop, step by step, and breath by breath, defeat the ego. The ego is destined to dissolve, as it is a foreign element. The weakest point of the ego is in its inability to persist for extended periods.

THIS TOO SHALL PASS

It appears energies, which have certain levels of charges, will eventually get discharged if they're not reacted to and allowed to feed on your emotions. The principle of patience is based on allowing the ego to discharge and evaporate. It is best never to act or react at any time to anything influenced by the ego. It is healthy not to answer phone calls immediately, as it is the ego who would suggest to you the importance of the call and would do it to your disadvantage. Let it ring a few times, and then answer. Better still, do not answer the call, but return it after a few minutes. Phone messages and emails should be dealt with in the same manner. It is highly prudent to delay everything for some time as practically as possible. We face life situations and their consequent challenges continuously, and we may need to respond to situations fast. No one is exempt, not even the most powerful of all. It is the promise of the divine. It is the divine approach to strengthen your back, wake up, discharge the ego, and distance yourself from it. Patience will avail the necessary time and space to overcome any adversity. It is also the divine promise that any adversity will invariably pass if you give time and patience.

A tale was told by Rumi and Attar, Sufi poets. The fable reads like this: A poor young scholar is wandering in the Maranjab Desert and has no place to sleep and eat. A well-off farmer offers the young man shelter and food, but on his departure, when the young man asks about the farmer's kindness and hospitality, his response is "This too shall pass."

Years pass, and the scholar visits the farmer, only to find him poor and disheveled, working as a low-grade servant. Floods have destroyed his prosperous lands, but not fretting, he tells the scholar, "This too shall pass."

The scholar ages and becomes famous and well renowned in the area and moves back to the Maranjab Desert. The king at the time, who has lost his wife and son during childbirth, is thoroughly depressed, crying himself to sleep every night. He seeks out a ring that will cheer his spirits and appease his suffering. People from all over try, but nothing of importance resonates with the king. Then the scholar, now not so young, is sought out to advise the king and perhaps suggest a phrase. Shortly thereafter, a gold-and-ruby ring appears from the scholar with a phrase inscribed inside: "This too shall pass."

EGO SHOPPING

When you are tempted to make a decision, particularly when buying items, if you delay your decision for a day or two, you may find that it was not necessary, and the need was triggered by the ego. The ego will drive you to make decisions and take actions on its behalf, particularly when you are tired, hungry, ill, or upset. Avoid going to a marketplace for food shopping when you are hungry; if you go when hungry, you will end up buying twice what you need, if not more. Dress up in your best attire when going to shop for dresses, or you will buy anything more elegant than what you are wearing at the time. Delaying and having patience are useful strategy to avoid deciding and taking action on behalf of the ego. Even when eating food, make sure you are not eating for your ego. In every choice, every selection, and every decision you encounter, the ego will be there for you to take its share. Peter Donaldson, English author of the book *Economics of the Real World*, states that 80 percent of our needs are ego-induced needs and are not our actual needs. The ego provokes these pseudoneeds through thoughts that drive you to compare yourself to what others have, not what you really need, or to have things to impress people you actually dislike.

The delay-and-patience strategy will help you to a great extent to formalize your affairs to your best interest, not to satisfy stupid emotions. These strategies can be strengthened when coupled with conscious breathing and sense perception. The ultimate aim is to stop or reduce your ego-induced thinking. That is not your thinking; it is done to you. When you reach any level of awareness, you are conscious to that level, which enables you to observe the play of ego in yourself and in others.

IDENTIFICATION WITH EGO-INFLUENCED NEEDS

When the ego is at play in your thoughts, it gets you to buy things that are not your needs. Marketing and advertising specialists are highly aware of this tendency in you and are good at getting into your mind to make you buy things you don't need and at much higher prices than they are worth. How does this game work? They know that the majority of people are under the influence of their egos. This makes them susceptible to external suggestions that trigger false desires. One of the most potent desires is the ego-induced desire to stand out or to be like those who stand out, such as the famous, celebrities, influencers, or successful individuals in all fields. Or it's just a matter of feeling that those things will add something to how you feel yourself or want to be seen by others and add more worth to your stance in general. Marketers will suggest to your unconscious mind that by using a certain product, you will be seen as a distinctive person, reaching to what you think you are. Or they may do the same thing to create some linkage in your mind with a famous person, who could be an actor or actress, sportsperson, model, or successful executive or entrepreneur, by some intricate psychological marketing and promotion techniques. They succeed in convincing you that when you buy or wear the product, you will become like those people in advertisements. You are enhancing an identity and buying an illusion of success or fame that satisfies your ego for sometimes. Designer or signature items are targeted to pull you into the game and give a boost of self for a short period time. These items are sold at inflated prices that not everybody can afford, so they are exclusive; thus, you become exclusive. The major part of the price constitutes the psychological value of the item, which, undoubtedly, evaporates within a season or shorter, depending on the ego's demands. Then you are left with their material value.

Gibran said, "Don't make your clothes most expensive thing about you, lest you find yourself one day worth less than what you wear."

EGO DRESSING AND BOOSTING

This narcissistic tendency is not uncommon and can be seen in all walks of life. You can easily identify these people. They usually are overly elegantly dressed, wearing glittering accessories, such as gold watches, branded belts, and expensive rings or neckless. They look perfectly neat, perfectly in place for attention and admiration from anyone they come across. They watch and calculate the amount of self-value they reap from each encounter, presence, and show. They gain a feeling of joy and gratification for some time, but it is always a short time. Then the cycle must repeat, as the ego always wants more. In some cases, this tendency repeats incessantly, producing addiction and leading to depression, self-pettiness, and self-destruction. It can never be a winning situation, because real self-worth is within and cannot be derived from external forms.

The personal outfit is only one item narcissists hook into. They also focus on their houses, cars, offices, restaurants they go to, social circles, and political or business groups. This type of narcissistic behavior is also found among educated and intellectual individuals who attempt to stand out by disseminating their knowledge in a showing-off manner, attempting to say, "I know, and you don't know," or "I know more than you know." Some use sophisticated language in their talks and speeches to make sure you don't understand what they say, giving you sense of inferiority and making themselves superior to you. I have observed a similar narcissistic tendency in a few spiritual teachers and coaches, who expose their self-created rank among others and use sentences in their speeches and books that can only disturb what good and useful knowledge you already have. Einstein said if you cannot explain a subject to a child, then you don't understand it yourself. This is true with many speakers and authors.

Narcissistic behavior is wasteful, harmful, and defeating to the narcissist and to others in all cases. This no-win situation draws the narcissist to melancholy and self-shrinkage, which is precisely contrary to the main aim sought.

COLLECTIVE NARCISSISM

Collective narcissism implies collective unconsciousness and collective irrationality. *Collective* means many people gathering regularly in common places, such as workplaces, marketplaces, and schools, for collective common purposes. These places are production-oriented and settled. However, over time, they develop collective behavior they become identified with. For example, workers in manufacturing companies tend to be highly disciplined and industrious and have somewhat inflexible manners. Children in private schools tend to be more open- and liberal-minded. This applies to many other similar places. There is a common feature of the people gathering in each of these places: they have their own behavioral profile that makes them work in a coherent and harmonious work style to achieve common goals. This tendency is healthy and necessary. If these people need to go on strike, then they behave in the same cooperative motion but in the opposite direction. The ringleaders are skillful in exploiting the collective tendency of this type of human gathering to serve ulterior intentions. It is conveniently possible, in these conditions, to rally people, although they may not be conversant with the cause and purposes of the movement. Nevertheless, because of their collective, intertwined minds, they go a long way to exert their efforts to impact the proceedings of the events, which inadvertently go in an unpeaceful direction progressively, gathering momentum and leading to life-threatening violence and destruction.

Building a collective mindset for any noble reason is prone to go in the opposite direction. Conscious intervention can play a critical role to keep the motion from taking a detour, by rehabilitating the mindset to a more alternating mind mode, rather than a fixed mode. That is usually achieved through special behavioral reconditioning. This necessitates much consciousness and presence.

COLLECTIVE DISGUISE

Collective narcissism is more potent when the human gathering happens at the mind level through ideologies, dogmas, religions, propaganda, or just pure irrationality. The media for this gathering, in the distant past, were preaching, teaching, and lecturing or written rituals.

Souk Okaz, the Okaz bazaar in Mecca, was one of the oldest places where people gathered to exchange written works of literature in the period of AD 542 to 726. The works of literature were mostly written in the poetic Arabic language and presented on animal skin or papyrus as pendants or murals, mostly narrated by the originators. The Arabs of the time somehow were aware of the hypnotic effect of the poetic form of written narrated literature. The classical Arabic language is intricately tuned to create rhythms and is voiced slightly forcefully through the throat, creating distinctive tonality that is hypnotically potent. Reciting Koranic verses, hitherto, is always rhythmic and harmonious. Some non-Muslims have reported their experience of the pull of listening to the recitation of the Koran even though they do not understand the Arabic language. A German man has a video showing him listening to a Koran recitation for the first time, and in it, he shows immense emotions, despite being nonconversant with the Arabic language.

A wider impact on reaching the masses emerged in 1436 with the advent of the printing press, invented by Johannes Gutenberg, which led to reaching more people. But the tipping point was in the first concerted and targeted endeavor, which gave birth to the first printed newspaper, the *Relation of Strasbourg*, published in Germany in 1605 by Johann Carolus. The newspaper's ulterior aim was to reach the largest masses and influence the minds, thoughts, emotions, and actions of the maximum number of people to adapt to certain dogmas with devotion, serving certain parties of interest. Today's media is more potent, pervasive, and exploitative than at any time in the past. As such, it has induced further and deeper unconsciousness in the minds of increasingly more people, disguising their will and abusing their affairs. Today more people are living more irrationally, more destructively, and more absurdly than at any time in history. If you think otherwise, you are traveling at a high speed without a safety belt.

Modern mass media has been distinctively capable of deceiving and misdirecting the choices and decisions of a great majority of people, pulling them into deeper irrationality that has become their compulsive and obsessive behavior, which is madness.

Masses who stand in open spaces in cold weather for long hours, reacting to a popular singer hysterically, display madness. Masses who travel across countries, incurring high expenses of money and time, to watch a football match and possibly return disappointed display madness. Masses who stand for hours and hours on both sides of the street, under exhausting conditions, to see a celebrity or a leader pass for a flying second display madness. Masses who spend hard-saved money to buy overpriced designer dresses and accessories to give themselves self-value, which only lasts for a few days, display madness. Masses who take part in demonstrations without knowing the cause and exert tremendous effort and time to eventually become violent and cause harm to others display madness. Masses who get absorbed into dogmas and follow them blindly, unwittingly, and willingly to the death display madness.

These and similar radical behaviors are reflections of the irrationalities that feed deeply hidden emotions, revealing the concealed dark side of human nature.

MADNESS AS A PROFESSION

Masses are oblivious to and disconnected from reality and act in irresponsible manner. Look around; where there is a crowd, you will see the consciousness of the individuals drop and their energies grow. They become daring and aggressive—a ticking time bomb. These individuals accumulate forces of radicalism, which become a personal, fixated trait whose main aim is to stay radically independent of the cause or subject matter. When such a person finishes with one cause or gets defeated or expelled, he or she will search for another to continue performing the lifelong profession. Cases have been reported in which these radical individuals have changed sides opposite to their earlier side. A radical religious activist broke ranks and joined a liberal movement, fighting against restrictions imposed by his former religious group. In both cases, the radical individual brings sacredness in whatever cause and radically fights for it, despite, in all cases, being ignorant of it.

NEED FOR COLLECTIVENESS

On another side, the human being is naturally attracted to joining others to satisfy the need for belongingness, as stipulated by Maslow in the hierarchy of human needs, and for assurance and emotional integration, as well as teamwork or collective endeavors. There is a good degree of comfort in being or functioning in a group, as we experience at work, in the family, or in social groups. The same condition is experienced in joining guided tours or missions. Being in a group is actually unavoidable in life, but it is critically important to safeguard yourself against the inevitable group pull of self-defeat and, potentially, self-retraction. It is possible and practical to be in and out of the group at the same time. Firstly, you should be fully aware that you are in a group, which is not always obvious. Secondly, you should be aware that a group has dynamics that are highly prone to going astray and causing damages in many directions. Thirdly, you should stay conscious all the time of your body and mind; practice presence through sense perception and conscious breathing continually. Understand that a group does not stick together for long; members change, and so does the loyalty of the individual. You may become a surplus. It is prudent to keep your trust in the group down.

CHAPTER 9

NATIONAL LEGACIES

GENEROSITY OF THE EGO

M Y COUNTRY, BAHRAIN, IS A small island 760 square kilometers in area, situated between Qatar and Saudi Arabia. In geographic proximity are Kuwait, United Arab Emirates, and Oman, and together they make the Gulf Cooperation Council (GCC). Within the same circle are Iraq and Iran. Not going farther northwest of the region, the physical living conditions within the circle are hot and harsh for at least six months of the year but now are made relatively comfortable and convenient by air-conditioning technologies and high-standard amenities. The GCC countries are oil-rich countries that enjoy some of the highest living standards and quality of life in the world. These countries are also called Gulf Arab countries, and the people of these countries are called Gulf Arabs. They are historically known for being overly generous to guests and the needy. Yet these countries, because of the environment, were, until recently, short on food and water resources. To be generous when you have enough is righteous and sensible, but to give when you do not have enough is ponderous and elusory. This social custom is still practiced in the region, even though the root cause of it has long disappeared. For example, the people of Bahrain have been ranked by international organizations as among the most giving nations in the world, and Bahrain has been ranked as the best destination for work and living for foreigners. In general, all Arab Gulf countries are receptive to other nationalities.

The present behavior of the Arab Gulf societies is a remnant of the past—a past that was harsh, painful, and dangerous. To survive in these conditions, the tribes made treaties to support one another for food security and physical protection against dangers. Although the outcome is noble and favorable, the root cause is now egoic. A fear of the past lingers in the deep self of the Gulf Arabs, and the ego is accessing and agitating the fear reservoir, causing unconscious generosity that has generated mounting waste.

Being conscious of the origin of the behavior is necessary to allow what is favorable to continue. Here the issue is a little complex: you want to continue with the behavior but need to disconnect it from its source, reformat it, and consciously redeposit it in the inner-self memory. Mass media can play a potent and constructive role in enlightening the masses through awareness and repetition. This reformatting can also be achieved on an individual level through stillness with concerted inner self-reflection.

This positive outcome of the negative source is different from dealing with destructive ego-induced behavior and is rarely talked about or dealt with, as it might not be a widespread feature of society and individuals.

NATIONAL DESTRUCTIVE BEHAVIOR

Destructive ego-induced collective behavior is vastly in action within many nations. These nations have endured the pain of wars, famine, natural disasters, injustice, suppression, torture, and insults. As a result, they have accumulated layers of pain body. That is why the older nations carry heavier burdens, have stronger pain bodies, and behave more irrationally, inflicting harm on others and themselves. The older nations are more prone to wars. Look back only a few years, and see which nations went to war in Yemen, Afghanistan, Bosnia and Kosovo, Iran, and Iraq, in addition to the never-ending Israeli-Palestinian conflict. These hostilities happened in recent time, when we think we have come to our senses. None of these wars and conflicts have brought any solutions, because there were no real causes. All the causes were related to the distant past emanating from their mostly dormant pain bodies, which do not resemble in any way the present realities. If you go to war for delusive cause, you will lose the war. That is like seeking solutions for problems that do not exist except in the mind. America and European countries are the most war-driven countries in the world, at least for the past five hundred years, going to war for the same ever-active, expired reasons. Countries that have the same pain bodies but intentionally diverted their pain-body energies into work and other constructive activities, such as sports, were able to desensitize their collective egoic pains, which have by far been mitigated.

Observing your national pain bodies is as important as observing your own and helps you not to be drawn to your dark side and follow intense rhetoric and national emotions.

TOUCHING THE DIVINE

Our mission in life is to reach our true selves, where happiness and peace are our innate traits. We all yearn to tear the veil that bars us from realizing divine bliss. Although it is always healthy to take the right path, the path of enlightenment, to reach the love of the real you, awareness is the key to salvation.

We all have experienced glimpses of awareness in restricted space and time. For some, these incidents opened a slit where the light of the divine penetrated the soul, creating a blissful sensation, which then was promptly concealed by the ego. Near-death experiences reveal the power of divine love, and those who return to life do not want to. At that time, near-death people drop their false selves. Dropping the false self in mundane life is the ultimate hope of humanity.

We strive in many different ways to reach the destination, which is only one destination. We choose a vehicle most relevant to us, which is not necessarily a universal vehicle. All religions lead to the same destination. All spiritual teachings help you to that destination. All the cracks in your life are the ways to that destination. All these approaches are aimed at losing your false self. The means of the journey to the divine is best chosen consciously. The journey may be long for some and short for others, but it is a sustainable joy that grows along the way. People who choose, probably unconsciously, to only have glimpses of the divine touch for a moment or two are destined to repeat it, but every time, it is only a glimpse of the touch; it never adds up or grows. It may become addictive and compulsive. This type of journey will never reach the destination.

Rupert Spira, an English spiritual teacher, philosopher, and author, explains the glimpses of losing self in multifaceted real-life situations. Spira says that on a trip to Amsterdam for a conference, he had a short tour of the nearby city square. He saw a bungee-cart Playfair activity in a small park. People paid money to be taken thirty meters up and then plunged in a high-speed swirling motion. They were taken up a few times. The people in the bungee carts were intensely frightened and screaming. Then the bungee stopped, and the people came out smiling and immensely relieved. Spira explains that these people were invoking, willingly, a heightened fear of death in themselves, dropping all resistance to life and totally surrendering to the near-death situation. In that situation, for a moment or two, they lost their false selves and vanished, freeing the true self. Then nothing mattered, which gave them a glimpse of a sensation of happiness and peace.

The second place he visited was a church on another side of the square. Inside the church, people were in a state of complete stillness, serenity, and reverence. They were losing themselves in God. They too were divorcing themselves from their false selves, as the people in the bungee carts were, but for a little longer, enjoying a longer sensation of happiness and peace.

A short distance away from the square, Spira went through a few narrow streets that led him to the Red Light District, to a brothel. Seeing what went on around the place, he gathered that people who came there came to lose their false selves and experience their true selves for a moment or two, at the time of aroused orgasms. Contrary to popular belief, they were not there for the fun of sexual pleasure.

The three places—the bungee fair, the church, and the brothel—led people to lose their false selves and find their true selves. Three different places, with three different proceedings, led to the same destination—regretfully, for a short time.

The people, due to the short spell of real happiness, normally go back and repeat the experience. The repetition eventually creates a compulsive need for and addiction to the substance or the source. Even meditation, under compulsive pull, is addiction. Prayer, under compulsive devotion, is addiction. So are physical exercise, intellectual indulgence, and many other seemingly upstanding activities. Short spells of real self-realization do not contribute to increasing the consciousness level in an accumulating manner. They are always little for a short time and never add up or grow, which inevitably makes way for the ego to invade and activate more pain bodies. However, if you are aware of the nature of this motion, it is not bad to go for physical and social enjoyment in the right places. It can help you to release your stress. Unfortunately, most people who resort to these motions are unaware and mostly inflict harm on themselves and enlarge their false selves. The same effect can be obtained from alcohol and narcotics. If they're taken beyond medical measures, addiction and self-destruction are inevitable. But we all know that in all cases mentioned, it is unrealistic to assume people can stick to the right measures. At the outset, these sources normally give you some relief from your mind at the high price of your dropping eventually below the thought and losing consciousness.

SOCIAL GATHERINGS

In a social gathering, we find comfort from a sense of belonging and a sense of security for some time. It helps you to dissociate from your mind by listening to others. This is an audio-sense perception. Audio-sense perception is best practiced by listening to the sounds produced in nature, such as the sounds produced by sea waves, the wind, or the trees. They are healthy sounds because your mind does not interact with them and, hence, does not produce perceptions that provoke thoughts. This leads the mind into deeper stillness and heightened consciousness.

In social gatherings, although your mind experiences such relief for a moment or two, then it goes to the minds of others and draws thoughts from them, just like plugging into other sources of egoic thoughts. Now your mind has been taken over and run by others. In these situations, you tend to drag on in the gathering until it is over. Normally, people find it hard to leave the gathering before the end of it, because their minds are hooked to and intermingled with one another's egoic thoughts, lowering their consciousness. With some social groups, the gathering is repetitive and for longer periods, not because anything of interest or importance arises but precisely because there is nothing of interest to talk about. At this stage, the group develops a collective ego, which is far stronger than the total sum of the individuals' egos, and develops group egoic self-identity. The group develops a general tendency to agree on negative subjects and quarrel over positive ones. The more trivial and meaningless the subjects are, the more addictive they become.

If the talks are useful and interesting, they become thought-provoking and stimulate individuals' minds to think for themselves, which is much more useful than a group-induced trance, and individuals' attention is not held captive by ambience. We cannot avoid group gatherings, nor should we, but we should consciously choose to use the group ambience to induce more awareness and presence.

TV AND SOCIAL MEDIA

Watching TV and scrolling through social media are more distractive because the content is mostly targeted and intended by the agents and parties of interest to create a hypnotic effect on your thoughts, so their thoughts become your thoughts; hence, you behave their way to their interest, even if it's possibly harmful to you. Most TV channels and social media servers are controlled by people who are intensely controlled by their egos; hence, all have hidden agendas to control you, put you in hypnotic mind mode, make you unconscious, and rally the herd like sheep.

However, the content of TV programs and social media uploads, when there are certain factual qualities, like social gatherings, can serve to awaken you, energize your mind, and raise your awareness. Programs such as documentaries and docuseries; some movies; and the sites of intellectuals, scientists, and spiritual teachers have produced massive positive effects on people and transcended their presence and consciousness.

It is profoundly prudent to avoid frequent and prolonged TV watching and social media scrolling. They drop your consciousness, increase passivity in you, and sabotage your energy.

---- ⟲ ----

CHAPTER 10

HAPPINESS

HAPPINESS WITHIN

HAPPINESS IS ONE OF THE seven traits (along with love, peace, purity, wisdom, knowledge, and power) embodied in you at the moment of your inception in the womb, and it is your main purpose in life. The strength and size of your happiness, which is the same for all people, remain constant throughout your life. No one can add to or take away from your happiness in any way. Happiness is not affected by external forms, such as your belongings and status, or your mind-made self. It is there for you all the time if you help it manifest for you. Happiness is an absolute state of being; its opposite is not unhappiness but the absence of happiness. Unhappiness is a fictitious state of mind created by the false self, which is totally irrelevant and foreign to happiness. There is a source in the universe that emanates happiness, but there is no such source in the universe for unhappiness, which is better called *misery*, to sever its mind-made link with happiness. A similar relationship exists between light and darkness. The source of light in the solar system is the sun, but there is no such source for darkness anywhere. The light is absolute and has no opposite; darkness is just a positioning effect that veils the light. If you travel eastward at the right speed all the time, you will never experience darkness. Equally, if you travel inward into your inner self all the time, you will always encounter happiness and never meet unhappiness.

ROCKING HAPPINESS

During the 1980s, I was working as a member of the management team of a large manufacturing company. There was a maintenance contractor who did masonry and hygiene work for us. The contactor had many supervisors, and one of them was a childhood friend of mine, whom I did not have regular contact with. He visited me in my office one day, and while we were talking about general social subjects, for some reason, I gathered that he was not adequately paid, and I was not sure if he lived his life comfortably enough. I decided to find out what I could do to help him improve his financial condition. A couple of ideas came to my mind: to find a suitable job for him in the same company I was working for or to help him with what he needed but could not afford. We had a common childhood friend I decided to bring into the matter. Together we decided to visit our unfortunate friend in his residence, which was in an area called Essa Town, which was originally built by the government for low- or limited-income citizens. The town had many sizes of houses and apartments to suit family sizes. The houses were mortgaged for extended periods with nominal repayment amounts. The apartments were for rent for next to nothing. My friend was living in one of these apartments, so naturally, I gathered he had a very low income. On a weekend night, our common friend and I decided to visit our friend in his apartment.

We arrived at a confined square with a small park, where some children were playing football. Others were racing around the square. The level of noise was astonishingly high and reverberated a great deal of joy and liveliness. A small boy approached us and asked if we were going to park where we initially stopped and suggested politely that we park our car farther up on the right corner. We parked the car, and the little boy gave us a thumbs-up. I still can recall a snapshot of the boy: he had wide black eyes, a sweaty tan face, a vigilant body posture, and an innocent smile on his face. The boy was fully happy by divine standards.

We went into the four-story building and climbed the stairs two floors to reach the apartment. All the way through, the surroundings were basic, neat, and somewhat dull, which did not give any indication of reasonable well-being. We reached the door of the apartment and did not ring the bell for a while. We both glanced at a small piece of salt rock hanging on the door, which was intended to deter evil eyes and to absorb negative energies. I guess it is practiced in other parts of the world. We both smiled blissfully. We rang the bell, and the daughter opened the door. She was around twelve years old, wearing a Walkman with headphones, flicking her fingers to the music she was hearing. She just looked at us and gave us a nod, suggesting we come in. The son, on the other side of the entrance hall, was busy playing with a small bouncy ball, jumping and twisting while trying to catch the ball in hit-and-miss trials. Our host and his wife welcomed us pleasantly and warmly, more than a usual greeting. They escorted us to the living room. The furniture was basic; there was no sofa. We sat on the floor, on an old carpet that looked like an old nomadic Persian carpet. The wife served us tea in traditional cups called *estikan*, small glass cups narrowed in the middle. Some are plain glass, and others have paintings engraved on them.

After a while, our host pulled out stacks of video cassettes. He explained he had Egyptian movies dating back to our childhood period. Egypt was, and still is to some degree, the Hollywood of the Arab world. Then he suggested we watch an old movie called *Alseraa Ala Elneel* (*The Clash on the Nile*), featuring Omar Sharif and his wife, Fatin Hamama. He had many old movie cassettes.

The daughter came in with a game board. I did not understand, but we all were pulled to play. The game involved throwing dice and collecting points on the dice's faces. I did not win but had great fun. We all laughed at how you can win time and again but lose it all in one go. The atmosphere was full of joy, fun, and kindness.

The wife threw a table sheet onto the floor in the middle, saying it was dinnertime. The meal was modest and warmly spiced with kindness and love.

We left the apartment pleased. I was thinking about finding my friend a better job and possibly gifting him with pieces of furniture. However, while we were going down the stairs, my accompanying friend, surprisingly, said to me, "Do not do anything for this man and his family. Do not disturb their life. They are happy—happier than you and me. They shared some of their happiness with us tonight. They do not need our help; we need their help."

They already had everything they needed to be happy, and that was why they had the salt rock on the entrance door to protect them from evil eyes. Traditionally, we expect that the salt rock is used by people who own large houses and have high-value items. That was why we smiled at the salt rock on the main entrance door, as if saying, "What high-value belongings could they have that need protection?" My accompanying friend told me the family had a high-value life and happiness that needed protection against evil eyes.

When you are happy, don't rock the boat, and don't let anyone rock it for you. You may think rocking the boat means sailing and going distances, while it is destabilizing your life and your consciousness. Eventually, it will sink the boat or make your life rock all the time.

The happiness we seek is already in us. No one and nothing can ever give it to us or take it away from us. It is correct to improve your financial condition to better your comfort and convenience in all affairs of your life but not to expect doing so to bring you happiness. Even your comfort and convenience, when they are obtained, should not be detrimental to the quality of your life. Enjoy them, but never get attached to them. Attachment is a vice that makes you deny your innate value of your true self. When you have the comfort and convenience of life, enjoy them, but when you don't have them or lose them, still enjoy your time as if you have them. When you wish for something, live as if you have it. In doing so, you create the right energy field to attract it. The converse is true too: feeling deprived by not having something or losing something will create a negative energy field that will repel it for you. For happiness, fortunately, you do not need to do anything; just allow it to manifest by being aware and conscious. The happiness you are seeking is seeking you more earnestly. Your job is to calm your false self in the way that is most workable for you. Two ways available all the time everywhere are conscious breathing and sense perception.

DUALISM

In general, the situation of mankind is dysfunctional and regretful. Most people inflict pain on themselves and others, albeit mostly unconsciously. People lie to each other, steal from each other, usurp each other's rights, envy each other's successes, and enjoy each other's failures, and worst of all, people pretend they love each other. Human insanity has reached diabolic proportions. In most so-called civilized and progressive societies, atrocious acts of inhumanity take place. There is no sense in attacking kindergartens and schools and killing young children. There is no sense in paying money to go to boxing matches to watch two human beings inflict injuries on each other and call it entertainment and sport. There is no sense in seeing human beings being tortured or killed only because of their skin color, race, or religion or just because they're not alike. Then the same human beings take on massive movements to promote human rights, equality, protection of children, inclusion of the disadvantaged, eradication of poverty, and so on. What are the causes of these contradictory acts of human behavior?

If creatures from outer space came to visit us on Earth, what do you think they would say about human beings? Would they say we are kind to each other? We love and care for each other? We care for the animals and other species living with us? Do we protect the environment?

MANIFESTING TRUE SELF

People are rarely who they portray themselves to be. To varying degrees, people wear masks and change their skins all the time, except for brief spells of awareness imposed by life situations or induced by deliberate acts of awakening. What they conceal is the false self, and what they portray is another false self. They are falsifying the false. Humanity is now trapped in this situation, which is oscillatory self-falsification.

A moralist preacher who spends much of his time preaching morality and then is caught sexually molesting young children is a typical case of oscillatory falsification of self. In his deep, true self, he is aware that his practicing of morals is irrelevant to the reality of life. Also, like all of us, he has a mind-made self made of his experiences in life and accumulated memories. The moralist preacher is actually responding to the egoic desire, forming a concealing layer—acting with a mask on—for whatever the ego needs through theatrical plays. He falsifies the role in the play and commits a compromising act contrary to his falsified true self. In other situations when actors, such as preachers, moralists, reformers, and social activists in all walks of life, call for forbidding certain acts or intentions, when they, behind their masks, do not believe in what they say, they either want them exclusively for themselves or believe that since they cannot have them, no one else should have them. Gibran offered a parable on this falsification, saying that an aging snake that cannot change its skin anymore climbs on a platform and accuses younger snakes of indecency and shamelessness.

These tendencies are also often seen in revolutionary political opponents who marshal the masses to fight against wrongdoing that they commit later. Gibran also said that the opposition does not stand against the acts of injustice or wrongdoing the incumbent regime commits but struggles to usurp the power only to commit the same.

Maximilien Robespierre rose to power during the French Revolution and managed to oust what was called the old and unjust regime. Under his reign, executions peaked like never before. In four months, twenty thousand people were put under the guillotine, and the economy of France slumped to its worst performance compared to the last twenty years before revolution, when it had been at its best performance. Gibran neatly put it this way: "Our wrongdoings take precedence over yours." This is what the opposition say in their real hidden desires.

ACTIVE DENIAL IS ACTIVE DESIRE

In moralistic, political, work, and other arenas of life, oscillatory falsification can be detected when people voice their stances a little higher than needed and unnecessarily repeat them. The executive narcissist leaks this falsification more obviously than others. When there is a call for denial of some thoughts or acts, watch the callers closely. More likely than not, you'll discover they do not mean what they call for. We deny or forbid what we want. In essence, denying or forbidding is an act of resisting, and invariably, what you resist persists. According to Freud, the only way that something unpleasant or uncomfortable in our subconscious can reach our conscious mind is through active denial. We all express the very opposite of what is buried within us. We try to suppress our feelings, emotions, and actions, only to lose the grip in an embarrassing situation.

Denying and forbidding cannot work. Worse still, the denied feelings gather stronger momentum. The neuroconfiguration of the brain does not have a processing program for negating words or sentences. It cannot process subtraction or division; it can only process addition and multiplication. When you say to somebody, "Don't smoke," you remind him of smoking. Here the brain throws out the word *don't* because it has no program to process it. Many signboards on the streets or in public places produce the exact opposite of the intended effect. For example, with the message "Don't speed," at best, the driver will not reduce speed, but that is not what the sign was intended to achieve, and the driver is still hooked to speed, because the sign reminded him of the speed. Parents know that children repeat what they are told not to, and they do it for the same reason. If you tell a child, "Don't spill milk on the floor," the child will take it as "Spill milk on the floor," so it doesn't work. In workplaces, there are incalculable signs, messages, and written documents that disseminate negating instructions that only make people oppose them or, at best, ignore them. The best way to send a deterrent instruction anywhere is to convert the message to an equivalent positive command. For example, say to the child, "Drink the milk," or "Keep the floor clean," or divert the mind to something else. In the same manner, if I tell you now while you are reading this book, "Don't think of your hair," you will think of your hair for as long as you want not to think of your hair. To achieve this command, I tell you to think of your hand. When you think of your hand, then you don't think of your hair. Mission accomplished.

BIRDS IN OUR MINDS

In a management development program, we asked the participants to write ten lines of work practices they wished to improve and set the time to finish the task in twenty minutes, with one condition: while writing the lines, they must not think of birds. In the end, no one could avoid thinking of birds. Some said birds were everywhere; others said birds were jumping in their minds all the time.

You may use negative instruction in life-threatening places, enforcing the instruction by using force, physical barriers, and physical deterrents. But the mental deterrents remain elusive.

Observing your false self and its dynamics is the right path toward accepting your handicaps and fallacies. No one solves a problem if it's not perceived as a problem. Denying or forbidding a fact is a vice that directs to the road to peril paved with flowers.

HOMECOMING

The ultimate inner purpose of your life is to awaken. It is a shift in consciousness when egoic thinking and inner self-awareness depart. It is a progressive flow of consciousness that transforms every perception of life into the divine truth. This transformation is not an event but a gradual process most people undergo.

The first crack in the boundary wall of the awakening happens by a blissful force. It does not happen by practicing or following certain sets of steps or rituals. We have no say in it, and there's nothing we can do about it. Any attempt to induce the initial crack of awakening is an attempt to foster the ego to awaken itself, creating pseudoawakening in your mind—more play of unconsciousness. This opening can happen to anyone irrespective of the person's morality or spirituality. It can happen to a criminal or may not happen to a holy man; it is all irrelevant. The divine guides whom it wills.

BLISSFUL CRACK

In the past, it was popularly accepted that those who had weaker egos and lower levels of unconsciousness were more prone to have the blissful crack happen to them. Conversely, those who were more intensely unconscious were more intensely removed from having the initial crack. This understanding has been unfounded. There have been cases, albeit rare ones, in which people with intense unconsciousness experienced sudden and profound awakenings that transformed their lives dramatically and later left their imprints on the lives of millions of people in the world. In most cases, the crack happens in a more settled manner, wherein the individual suddenly becomes aware of his or her thoughts and starts the process of awakening, which cannot be reversed. However, it can be interrupted or slowed down occasionally by the ego.

Those who have found interest in listening to or reading material on self-development or spirituality have the initial opening happen to them. I once gave a book on spirituality—a world book I read three times and still study regularly—to a friend to read, but he could not find it comprehensible or useful at all. Obviously, the crack had not happened to him, and by implication, he had not entered the awakening process. For some, the initial crack happens when they become tired of their incessant negative thoughts jumping up and down like monkeys in their minds. Suddenly, they encounter the first glimpse of awareness that can recognize thought as thought and not as reality.

Now there is a space in the mind that may have thoughts in it but does not matter anymore because this space is conscious of the thought and is not part of it. The process will continue for the people who are experiencing it and are now able to be aware instantly of the thought and choose to allow it to pass rather than indulge in useless mind-thought mingling.

AWAKENING FOR AWARENESS

The awakening continues to induce awareness, which allows the presence to be experienced and create space in the mind. This space makes you see the significance of the emerging consciousness that sheds its light on the world and on your true understanding of the world.

When you experience awakening consciousness, almost everything in life appears different and has different meaning. Perhaps nothing has changed in the world, but your perception of it has become real. The narcissist executive you work for still behaves irrationally and may never change, but you no longer are receptive to his harmful and agonizing dysfunction. You will look at him as a child going on a rampage and see monkeys jumping all over his mind. Now you are awakened and conscious. You no longer react; you understand the ego play and possibly go laugh covertly, as you do with a child. In the same way, you will deal with other difficult people—maybe your parents, your spouse, your friends, people of authority, or just an intensely unconscious person on the road. Nothing has changed in the world, but everything has changed in the inner you, which changes everything in the world for you.

People who go through the process of awakening become gradually and progressively immersed in their inner true selves and become uncertain of their outer life and its purpose. What goes on in the world no longer impresses or influences them. Opening to the world, they see the insanity of mankind, and they may feel displaced from the social and cultural customs and practices. Some of these converts experience self-imposed isolation. Although they are aware of the ego play, they have not yet fully grasped the awareness in their lives. The inner and outer awareness has not yet synchronized.

CHAPTER 11

BEING AND DOING

HUMAN FUNCTION

A s HUMANS, WE HAVE MANY functions to perform in this world. One of the major functions is to contribute to the continuation of humanity by breeding children for the world. Other functions we have include interacting with other humans, other species, resources, and the environment to create further advancement in the world to meet the universe's expanding motives. These functions are performed in the outer world, the physical domain. Whatever you do at any given time is your purpose at that time, which is always the present time. We cannot do anything in the future or redo the past, because they do not exist. We may think we consciously decide to do things, but everything is commissioned to us by the divine or the source of the universe or God, except when it is induced by the ego. By God or by the ego, we remain serving agents or mediums or instruments of actions. We receive the commands and execute them accordingly, believing we are in command of our actions. We take good actions if the commands are from the divine or bad actions if they're from the ego. All the information, knowledge, ideas, life skills, inventions, innovations, discoveries, and solutions are transmitted to us by the divine to disseminate in the world. A simple parable to this effect is the TV set, which receives electronic signals through a dish or internet line, converts them into pictures and sounds, and then transmits them onto the screen and through the speakers. We cannot say the programs or the news we watched on the screen were produced by the TV set. They were all produced and broadcast by the producing and command center. Human beings cannot produce anything from their origin, just as the TV set cannot produce anything that comes onto the screen or through the speakers.

The human being, while receiving and transmitting, faces massive and frequent disturbances from the mind-made interpretations of perceptions caused by the ego. This is seen as madness on the screen of our civilization. On the TV screen, we watch interruptions and disturbances caused by the weather, a displaced dish, or a weak internet connection, but they are on a much smaller scale and are much faster to correct.

DIVINE COMMAND

In between your being and doing as a human being, ego creeps in and isolates you from the divine command center or disturbs your contact with your inner self, which is the reception center of the command center of the divine, or you may call it the soul. As long as the divine commands are improperly tuned to your inner self, your being part cannot function to the purpose of the divine. And as long as you are unaware of being, you will seek commands from the ego, which draws you to doing outside the present time realm—that is, doing for the future that does not exist. As such, any action or fulfillment you think you have accomplished will dissolve and vanish or turn out to be false and illusory. Any result we find in this situation is applicable only relatively and temporarily.

What do we achieve when we spend money, time, and emotions to watch a football match or any other competitive sports activity and offer our support to make our favorite team win by needing others to lose, fail, or be demeaned? The same goes for other external forms, such as status, wealth, fame, properties, clothing, and looks. I am not saying you should not have these in your life; on the contrary, you may have them for your comfort and convenience. However, do not identify your value with them or draw a sense of superiority from them, which, in any case, evaporates in a short time, as real superiority is never attained from external sources. You are already superior or, better said, complete and content. You are now as superior as the most superior person in the world, as both of you hold the same components of life and the same value, both of which are constant throughout your life. No one can add to them or take away from them. Only one factor can make you superior to others: the level of your consciousness. This factor resides in your inner self and can never be attained from external sources.

ALIGNMENT

It is paramount for our actions in the external world to be necessarily connected and aligned with the primary purpose of the inner self. Without this alignment, whatever we do or achieve is ego-driven. Even if it is grand and flamboyant, it will vanish sooner rather than later. Eventually, this will lead to distress and suffering, even if it is the noblest of motions or things. In the absence of alignment, ego will always be there to conduct you on how to do things, particularly when the things are positive, and will corrupt your thoughts and actions to do the right things in the wrong way.

Doing while being is, in the core realization, to be in the now, doing in isolation of time and divorced from entertaining anything in the future or digging into the ruins of the past. We merely need to negate the time that is always in the mind—that is, psychological time, or ego-made time. However, for life's practical purposes, we need to use clock time for making arrangements ahead of time to meet someone or planning to build a house. Planning is a job done in the present time, and subsequent actions are carried out in the now, according to the dates planned. Each date, when it arrives, will be dealt with as today, and the time is the present time, which is always now.

However, things go astray when we engage the mind in an attempt to seek achievement in the future. It is not there. We are forgetting that the only time when the action can be taken is the exact date and time scheduled, which, again, is always now. Once the plan is completed, whether to build a house or accomplish a task or a project, people usually start thinking about how the activities can go wrong. Or the budget falls short, the logistics get interrupted, and so on. But all these negative assumptions are the work of the ego and in the mind.

I spent more than twenty years practicing the management of work in an industrial complex where we always had plans for every sizeable task or project. Once the plan was made, at least once every week, we evaluated activities that would be carried out sometime in the future. This consumed our energies and resources so much that little was left to attend to the task at hand in the now. We always accomplished the projects on time and according to the plan or around it, but every time, we found that much of the energy, resources, and time were wasted in so-called project management on issues that were only in the minds and never appeared on the ground. I am not speaking here about a professional contingency plan; that is healthy to predict the probabilities of activities getting derailed or falling apart and that need predictive corrective action to be prepared ahead of the events. I am speaking about mind-made phobias of events that necessitate mobilization of massive amounts of resources but never happen. Yet the same proceeding is repeated for every new project. We called it *effective predictive project management* and sent the staff on expensive and long training programs to learn how to prepare to solve problems that did not happen on the ground. This is the same as a blind man looking in a dark room for a black cat that is not there. Many management practices are the work of the ego in the mind.

BLACK CAT IN A DARK ROOM

Management executives are obsessively engaged in looking for the black cat and creating solutions to problems they create in their minds. They are anxious most of their time in service, more anxious as they climb up the organizational hierarchy, always short of time and mind space, and somewhat dissatisfied. This applies to some entrepreneurs and wealthy individuals. This is an environment where the ego is strongly active, and the alignment between outer purpose and inner realization is severed. These people are efficient and effective in solving the problems they create. For 72 percent of the problems attended to, the solutions provided do not contribute value to the end products of the corporation.

It is healthier for management executives to align the primary objective purpose of the job with the actual actions taken and be aware of any forces of mind-made phobic requirements. Even if they produce masterpieces of work excellence, they will be corrupted in a short time, as they are the work of the ego, detached from the reality of work. Sooner rather than later, they will lead to degeneration of the organization, which often is blamed on external factors. Corporations that incorporate the practice of consciousness into their work and management styles have reported distinctive improvement in the well-being of the staff across the board and more so at the executive level. Also, they've reported increases in their output, with much-reduced efforts and resources.

When you focus on what you do and where you are, you dismiss the time on both sides of your mind. Past and future are abolished. This is a great relief from the burden of nonsense of life and creates alignment between your inner realization and outer forms, between being and doing. This focal point induces an enormous presence in what you do or where you are. Whatever you do, you will do it excellently, and it induces more consciousness and space in your mind, which in turn fosters more awareness and joy in your life.

AGONY, ANXIETY, AND STRESS

Among the most threatening dangers in life are those that do not exist in factual terms. In addition, most of our wants and needs are fictitious and also do not exist. Together they make life, for many people, miserable, agonizing, and excruciating. It is incomprehensible for many who experience mind-made problems to believe their suffering is caused by nothing.

A friend of mine has a young married daughter with two young children. He mentioned to me his daughter was suffering from worries and lack of sleep. One day he suggested I see her. Together with the father, they came to my house, and we had a brief talk about her condition. She did not talk about the causes of her condition. To make sure the condition was not caused by physical illnesses, I asked her about her general health and if anything was causing her sleep deprivation. There was nothing. Then I asked her what she thought the causes were. She mentioned her mother-in-law, who was living with them, was treating her with bad manners and aggression, and she constantly felt threatened by her. Then I asked her if the mother-in-law could actually harm her, either physically or morally. She said the mother-in-law was too old for any of that; she just had a big mouth. I then asked her if she would be bothered if the same talk that came from the mother-in-law came from a TV set or a radio. She paused and then, with a glimpse of shyness, said she would not be bothered. I went on to explain to her that she was not concerned with the content of the talk of her mother-in-law, and she agreed. Then I asked her to explain to me what was bothering her if it was not the content of the talk. She exchanged a few ideas, and I encouraged her to talk as long as she wanted. Finally, I asked her to pinpoint any one problem she was encountering. She replied that there were problems. At that point in time, I knew we'd reached halfway to the solution. Then I asked, if the mother-in-law was old and her talk was no more than rough, noisy talk we normally heard on the TV or the radio, what was causing the sense of threat to her?

She promptly said, "I am a fearful person."

Then I asked her to point to where the fear resided in her, and she pointed to her chest. In Arab culture, trapped emotions are usually believed to be in the chest. Now that she was aware of the root cause of her lack of sleep, I asked her to go home. I was almost sure a crack of awakening had happened to her that she needed to widen.

Two days later, the father called me and asked what I had done, as his daughter was now sleeping like a toddler. I said she had become aware of her mind-made egoic images of the threats, and the rest was her doing. This young mother had a pain body, possibly related to her childhood, that identified loud talk with threats. Becoming aware of that link severed or alleviated the association.

Like this young mother, millions of people in the world are disconnected from their inner selves, living fictitious lives full of fictitious problems.

FOSTER AWAKENING

Agony, anxiety, stress, and many more mind-made emotional conditions cause suffering, misery, and distasteful living conditions not because of justified life challenges but because of the absence of these challenges. Real challenges are the essence of being in the present time and consciously using the mind to create the desired conditions. The work you put into changing the conditions generates more physical and mental energies to the level you require. Conscious work is a bliss that fosters your awakening and your awareness and reconnects you with the source of the power of life itself, the source of the universe, or God. You are blessed if you are stricken at external levels and blessed because you are forced to consciously use your mind and take actions accordingly. In doing so, you have only one choice, which is to return to the source and be present. Agony, anxiety, and stress can never emerge in this situation, because they emerge and grow in time either future or past. Work and other challenges never produce agony, anxiety, and stress; these feelings are agitated by your perceptions of your surroundings and the people you deal with. These perceptions always are in the mind and only emerge and grow in the thoughts created by the ego. The ego turns them into images and fiction, which appear to you as living realities. Being challenged by a life situation is a blessing that can and will appear at times specific to your position in the universe. But that time is always now.

THE TRUE PATH

Now that you can turn inward to the source and stay with it for a longer period, as always, the living reality of the universe manifests for you every moment of your life. One small error, one misperception, creates havoc in your life for an extended period. Being conscious, aware, present, and connected with the source is taking the true and straight path. This path is not always furnished with flowers. You will meet the ego along the path to detour your journey. Remember that your journey is the journey of salvation, the journey of disconnecting with egoic thought, and the journey of understanding your purpose in life by reaching the source, or God. You do not need to comprehend God as a mental concept or a belief, because this God is a poor substitute induced by the ego. You require realization of the living reality of God.

IDOL DEITIES

God is in you, and you are an emanation of God. When we say the *love* of God, it literally means *oneness* with God. The mental concept of God created by the ego is the egoic God you fear. Anyone or anything you fear you cannot love; therefore, you cannot be in oneness with it. In the minds of many people are many ego-made gods. Some have been converted into stone-idol deities. Before the emergence of Islam, there were many idol deities made of stone and other materials in Mecca. These stone deities had rankings, and at the top were idols of deities called Lat, Manat, and Uzza. Before Islam, people worshipped these idols to no avail. Some of the idol deities were made of dates; people worshipped them in good times, and in famine times, they ate them. When Prophet Muhammad (PBUH) liberated Mecca, 1,400 years ago, his first command was to abolish and knock down all the idols, declaring that the widely pronounced verse in Islam "No God but Allah" means "No god but the God," a declaration of monotheism in Mecca. This task was relatively easy; however, the task of abolishing and knocking down idols in the mind is not easy. The mind is polytheistic and offers many gods, as many as the pain bodies individuals carry. In collective minds, the gods multiply to disproportionate limits like cancer cells, destroying the surroundings. Many spiritual and religious teachers are aware of the enormity of returning to one real source, the divine God. That is your inner self, where God is manifesting every moment of your life. Anything you listen to or pay attention to unconsciously becomes your fictitious god, except Allah, the God, or the source of the universe. Count how many gods you have: the god of fame, god of status, god of wealth, god of power, god of properties, god of movies, god of music, god of poems, god of fashion, god of football, god of narcissistic self, and so on. These gods or mental idols are made by your imagination, agitated by your ego. You not only believe in them, but you worship them with devotion. Many of the gods are short-lived, as is any desire created by the ego. Some linger for a long time. These gods, the pain bodies, and the memories can be eradicated. This is a scientific reality. The old notion that we are condemned by inherent genetic limitations and fixed intelligence is no longer valid. The popular present understanding is that the human mind is malleable and can alter itself in any way with persistence. Even genetic, hereditary malignant diseases have been cured by intense, elongated meditative focus. If you scratch the surface of a rock, you will eventually penetrate the depth of it. That is a parable we use in my society for persistence and devotion. Your agony, anxiety, and stress can all be eradicated much faster than you imagine. People who've experienced this approach have reported massive shifts in their consciousness in a couple of sittings. Others have taken relatively longer. Many have reported distinctive progressive openings in their awareness.

The process of awakening is timeless and endless. Shift in consciousness can come in many ways, but all need to be continued, because we are all laden with thick layers of accumulated memories—pain bodies—and as such, we all need to take on the process of cleaning up as part of our daily life routines and not call for special arrangement following set regimes of rituals.

AUTOSUGGESTION

Two techniques or tools were explained a few times earlier: conscious breathing and sense perception. A third one is autosuggestion, which is self-talk. This technique, like the former two, can be practiced anytime, anywhere, and in any circumstance and is profoundly impactful.

If you want to reprogram certain subjects in your memory portal storage that are creating disturbances to your well-being in general or causing you to react to certain situations unconsciously and embarrass yourself and others or if you want to transcend your handicaps and dysfunctions, this technique on its own can and should be used as part of your daily routine so it becomes a habit or natural tendency. It helps profoundly more if you perform the three techniques together. The principle of the autosuggestion is based on the fact that what you suggest to yourself through self-talk will get programmed in your memory to be called back intentionally by you or unconsciously by external triggers. You do autosuggestion for two main purposes. First, you want to modify information living in you that is unfavorable to your well-being—that is, delete and replace it. Second, you wish to develop certain tendencies and behaviors that do not exist presently in your functional memory but that you want to add and activate.

The basic principle works the same way for both purposes. Whatever you suggest to yourself will be picked up by your memory server and get autosaved in your memory for future activation. The memory body stores your suggestions and talk without judging or categorizing them. It does not distinguish between right or wrong commands or between serious or casual commands. It is necessary that you always use positive commands, even if you suggest avoidance of something. Your memory command center does not know how to command avoidance, because there is no action to call for. It just corrupts it. If people want to avoid being late, they usually say, "I will not be late." This command does not lead to any action, so it does not lead to generating energy in you. On the contrary, it will lead to inertia and inaction. That, in turn, will lead to more lateness. The energized command is to say, "I will be on time." *Will not be late* and *will be on time* do not have the same meaning. Your subconscious does not read your intentions; it takes your words literally. When, at times, you say something to yourself casually, such as "I bust," or "I am done," your subconscious takes it seriously and shuts you down. Or when you throw a joke at yourself, such as "I am a fatty jerk," for the sake of a laugh, it will program you to become fat and then a jerk.

Hopefully, you have now realized the sensitivity and vulnerability of words. Anchor your understanding to these dynamics of the words and sentences. "I will not be late" and "I will be on time" do not carry the same meaning and have opposite energy formation. Now you will be able to be conscious of selecting the right words and constructing energy-inducing sentences. For every negative word or sentence, there is a positive equivalent. As mentioned earlier, words like *no, don't, avoid, refrain,* and *stop* will deenergize your motions, and you will not respond accordingly. For example, if you suggest to yourself or raise a message saying, "No more overeating," the word *no* will not be processed, due to the neurological incapability and inaction. The effective, energized command would be "More balanced eating." Now you have something to do. Remember, I asked you earlier not to think of your hair, but you could not do it, because your hair was the object you neurologically could not disengage with. Then you disengaged with your hair by thinking of your hands; that worked well.

The same approach works effectively when suggesting not only to yourself but also to others that you need to do something and expect them to respond favorably. If you use force to command negative instruction, which is necessary in dangerous conditions, it works but only for a short period. Instead raising people's awareness to the ultimate aim of the command will give long and sustainable effects. Instead of the command "No way through" or "Stay away from this zone," use "Select another route."

BODY EXPRESSIONS

Primitive man did not have language to communicate with others for most of his history. Primitive humans were conversant with meaning that emerged on their faces and everywhere else on the body, as well as reading the pitches of vocalized voices. There were common body expressions for certain physical and emotional conditions. These expressions were produced and understood instinctively. Unlike verbal language, body expressions were universal. The body expression for love had a distinctive body posture and facial expression, and so did the body expressions for joy, contentment, sorrow, anger, fear, and the rest of human feelings and conditions. These body expressions are still produced and communicated but in unconscious manners we are mostly unaware of. Yet they have a sizeable impact on our interactions with each other. This impact amounts to 38 percent of the total communications between people; verbal communication using words makes up only 7 percent, and tonality makes up 55 percent, which I will explain later.

When you are joyful, your body exposes straightened posture, a raised neck, and a widened facial expression with a distinctive smile. When you are content, your body posture is more settled, not exposed and not retracted, and your facial expression is soothed and welcoming. When you are distressed, your body posture shrinks, your neck drops, and your facial expression is grouchy. When you are angry, your body posture is overcharged and tightened, your neck is extended forward, and your facial flares up. When you are fearful, your body posture is withdrawn, slightly trembling, and retreating. The same applies to many other bodily reactions you may observe but are not necessarily aware of. There are incalculable body and facial postures that express reactions to various perceptions of life situation challenges. More information on these postures and expressions can be found at www.scienceofpeople.com and www.verywellmind.com. These sites and many more help you to understand and learn the unspoken language of the body. This language enables you to understand other people as well as yourself in isolation of spoken language.

REVERSE EFFECT

The significance of body expression or language is that it works in reverse effect. For example, if you are sad and stand up in a joyful body posture—that is, you deliberately straighten your posture, raise your neck, and widen your face with a smile—sooner or later, you become joyful. The converse is also true: if you are joyful but for some reason make your body posture shrink, your neck drop, and your face scrunch, you will be distressed. The same effect applies to other types of body postures and facial expressions. Watching sad movies, looking at sad photos, or just seeing a sad scene anywhere will have this reverse effect on you, even though you might be in an opposite state. This is a serious call for being aware and conscious of your surroundings, body, and facial condition when the reverse effect is negative.

VERBAL LANGUAGE

The verbal means of communication is the most widely used means of communication between people and is the weakest of all. Verbal language is not instinctive, as are body language and tonality. Mankind did not have language for the longer part of his history. The Sumerian language can be considered the first language, dating back to 3500 BC, which makes it more than 5,500 years old. It was originally invented in Mesopotamia (modern-day Iraq). The sounds of all the letters of the alphabet of all languages exist in nature and among the living species. From these sources, human societies configured languages.

Verbal language is vulnerable and is highly and widely subject to misinterpretation, which can cause massive confusion and conflict among people. A word spoken is not necessarily a word we want to mean. A word spoken is not necessarily a word understood as meant. You might think this a simple problem humanity is facing, but consider this: 75 percent of the verbal and written communications received are misinterpreted; that is, for every one word understood, three words are misunderstood. This level of misinterpretation leads to similar levels of misunderstanding, making languages an impediment to harmonious human cohabitation. Conflicts between individuals, groups, and nations are mostly derivatives of misinterpretation and misunderstanding of the words communicated.

There are 7,117 languages spoken in the world. As mentioned earlier, spoken languages are not instinctive; they are widely influenced by societal cultures and individuals' comprehension. Conversing in more than one language is purported to increase understanding, but looking at only the first language alone and its confusing effect, we can see that any additional language, although it widens the communication sphere, will also offer confusing and conflicting costs. We all wish we could have one language to communicate with that is constant, in which the words are not open to interpretation, and there's one meaning for one word, but this is out of reach, at least for the foreseeable future. We are therefore faced with the challenge of learning to help one another for better understanding.

Words that are misinterpreted and misunderstood by others are also misinterpreted and misunderstood by our subconscious and memory storage; the ego loves this semantic handicap and fosters it. We need to be cautious in selecting words and making up sentences, more so for spoken than written communication and most importantly for communication with self, or self-talk, because you talk to yourself more than to anyone else, so your mind misinterprets your talk more than anyone else does. Therefore, the semantics of your words have a critical impact on your and others' behaviors. When you say to someone, "You are a liar," then you have condemned him for life, when what you wanted to convey was "You lied to me." The same applies to self-talk. You might say to yourself, "I am worried," which you can never be. However, the ego will receive it and make you believe you are, and it will stay with you. The correct way to convey this message to yourself is to say, "There is worry in me." The same applies to when you say, "I am angry," "I am doubtful," or "I am restless." These emotions you cannot be but can have. As such, the correct way to convey them is to say, "I have anger in me," "I have doubts living in me," and "I am experiencing restlessness." Here you are separated from your experience, which implies your experience is not you and is like a fleeting cloud, when you are the sky and are constant. Incorrect messages given to your mind will undoubtedly be picked up by your ego and charge your thoughts with false images of yourself that make your living conditions a nuisance and wasteful.

TONALITY

Tonality refers to the level and volume of emotions we put into the words we say, which transcend the literal meanings. Tonality, like body language, is instinctive. You do not learn it, but you practice it, mostly unconsciously. For example, when you are angry at someone but want to please him or her or want to show kindness, you say, "I love you." When you're in an angry mood, your voice is not tender and sweet, as it is when you are calm and caring. The tone of your voice in an angry mood is usually dry, hard, and forceful. The receiver picks up the tonality and translates the message not as its face value but as what you mean through the tonality of your talk. Dry, hard, and forceful talk is, we all sense, not talk that can express love. Invariably, we believe the tonality and not the words. Conversely, if you are not angry but have distaste for someone's behavior, say to him or her, "I hate you," quietly, hesitantly, and smoothly. In this mood, the tonality is tender, settled, and defused. The receiver picks up the tonality and does not take your words seriously.

The messages we convey need to have the right tonality attached to them to be comprehended accurately. At work, when the authorities issue commands or orders that the subordinates do not adhere to or respond to, it is because the tonality was inappropriate or showed leniency. In written commands or orders, the same tonality shows up in the use of inappropriate words. When the commands or orders are serious, they will not be taken seriously if soft and loose words are used in the text. When the issue is commanding, then words like "It is advisable," "It is preferable," "As circumstances allow," "It could be," and "It should be" are alien to the purpose of the message. Many professional analysts produce profoundly important and serious findings but present them in soft or hesitant tonality or writing, and as a result, they normally do not receive the right credibility and approvals.

TONALITY IS POTENT

It is essential that we become conscious of the tonality in our communication, both verbal and written, because its impact is tremendous and makes up 55 percent of the total volume of communication we do. An inappropriate tone or written word can turn messages upside down and can have dire consequences in our lives. Most conflicts are created by good intentions but wrong communication.

—— ⟋⟍ ——

CHAPTER 12

YOUR ROLE IN LIFE

SENSE OF DIRECTION

W E ARE ALL DESTINED TO take our role in life, but most of us are uncertain of the role and how to perform it. Animals have roles and rely on their instincts to lead them to fulfill their roles. Humans require some means of having a sense of direction, a way to guide and discipline our behavior in a semiautomatic mode of functioning. As humans, we are the only creatures who know we are mortal, and we are aware that our life span is limited by statistical spreads. Animals and other creatures do not have this awareness; they just die. We also are aware of the existence of incalculable species on planet Earth and of galaxies in the vast universe. Our position among all these cosmic dwellers incapacitates our existence on Earth. We are in constant search of some force to connect to that transcends us above our meager existence. We need to feel larger and more potent than we are and can be.

FICTITIOUS ROLE

The nature of our behavior is such that many people seek to create roles they think are going to give them a feeling of transcendence over the delusions that create misery, pain, and harm to self and others. These delusional roles seek to gain transcendence from external sources, such as status, fame, wealth, resources, and superiority, which eventually leads to false transcendence because external forms are not designed to and are unable to add or subtract any value for anyone. They do, however, create a great deal of grandiose physical exposures that give disguised images of transcendency and supremacy, which inevitably evaporate in time. The ego is the charged activator in these short-lived motions. It repeats them over and over again as each motion disappears or until the evitable consequence of self-degradation occurs, leading to depression and self-pettiness.

Real transcendence can only come from within, where all the value always exists and where only you can reach, where you and the universe meet. That's where the universe passes its purposes through you as an individual, as an important individual medium. You transcend from there, where the universe enables you to create and deliver ideas, paths, accesses, truths, and guidance to the world. It is a great mission to transcendence because it is from within; it is ours. No one and nothing from external sources have a hand in it. It is not a belief system that comes from outside you and is not influenced by others, who are deluded by their fantasies.

INWARD AND UPWARD

Real transcendence leads us inward and upward to a more being level through introspection and realization that help us to become empowered and enabled to contribute to human society. False transcendence leads us outward and downward to below consciousness level, which draws on the animal dark side of us, leading to grandiosity, fast-depleting abundance, depression, addiction, mental dullness, and cynicism.

We all, one way or another, fall into the trap of these delusional transcendences because they are outwardly attractive, easy to attain, and quick to show. It is critical that we become aware of these forces of false attraction and sever the ties with them. In this pursuit, we will be able to avail our nature of higher consciousness and transcendence.

FALSE PLEASURE

Over the course of our lives, one of our main pursuits is to avoid pain, primarily by seeking pleasure outside our true selves. The pleasures we seek may take different external forms, such as sex, alcohol, drugs, partying, gambling, eating, exaggerated shopping, expensive cars, overpriced attire, and compulsive spending on outings and holidays. In essence, none of these sources of pleasure are harmful in rational doses and periods. But when they are sought as pleasures to avoid pains, they turn into menaces, more so for people with high narcissistic tendencies. The effects of objects of pleasure trend toward diminishing returns and fast falls. People get trapped in situations where they ask for more with higher doses and insistently seek different stimulants. People become obsessed with the objects and disconnect from their true selves. The needs of these people drop down to the dark side of their selves, where the individuals are held hostage by their obsessive-compulsive cravings and addictions. At this juncture, the journey of self-destruction takes a toll on the lives of the people, whether they live while dying or their lives are cut short.

We all need pleasurable times outside work, family obligations, and social commitments. Pleasure and joy are effective means of relieving stress and tension. When we are aware of the purpose of pleasure and joy and consciously choose the correct times, we naturally know when to stop and limit the time and substance to the quality of the relief we seek, rather than overdosing and overstimulation.

FALSE BELONGINGNESS

Previous chapters explained collective unconsciousness and the corresponding ego dynamics and discussed the human need for belongingness and identifying with groups with shared notions and interests. A sense of belonging is a natural and healthy object of pleasure, joy, and affection because it serves the purpose of transcending the inner self through collective awakening. When individuals are unaware that the essence of belongingness emanates from within and emancipates outwardly, they seek pleasure, joy, and affection from external sources. It is like going out with an empty pot to be filled by others. This emptiness of the pot, or self-void, is easily and invariably filled with all kinds of beliefs, causes, and falsified truths and narratives, most of which are harmful and destructive. Then the need for group belonging turns into cult enslavement. In cult gatherings, the collective mind descends progressively and dangerously toward the lower dark side of the self. The worst cult is the religious military cult, which demands you follow their beliefs, or you will be severely punished. There are many types of groups that turn into cults and behave highly unconsciously. Less-violent versions of cults are seen in football and other sports, music festivals, political parties, racial groups, and even arts and literature societies. People who join groups or cults with an empty pot have nothing to offer to the group to create shared transcendence. These people have reached a point of near-total blockage of the inner self and have lost touch with nearly all their divine values. The group or cult does not attract individuals who value and want to develop themselves but attracts those who want to get rid of themselves altogether. On their part, they do not join a group or cult because they seek enhancement of self or transcendence of the collective, but they urge to become free of themselves; they want to get rid of themselves.

FIGHT FOR THE UNKNOWN

In cult groupings, the causes they raise and fight or even die for are kept vague, and group individuals must stay in that situation because they are empty of self. As such, they fight for what they do not know and lose interest as soon as they know. People in groups and large crowds are highly susceptible. By chanting rhetorical slogans repeatedly, one can become intoxicated and be made to swallow the most ridiculous and irrational suggestions. In such situations, individuals feel relieved of their personal responsibility, which normally leads to chaos, violence, and even killing. They feel they are enlarged and powered beyond their actual selves, when they are dwarfed and denied their will and their voice.

Joining groups or progressive movements that call for the reform and betterment of human life is a nebulous act of consciousness and transcendence above self that springs from our sense of responsibility toward life and people. Throughout history, many people devoted, risked, or sacrificed their lives—those who sought pleasure, joy, and affection in joining or leading groups or masses. This contribution must come from within and not out of a need to gratify our ego or just exhaust irritation.

WEALTH AND SUCCESS

Wealth is the amount of valuable material possessions, which include knowledge and intellectual materials, you own. In prehistoric eras, materials were exchanged based on mutual consent, such as "I give you grain, and you give me fish," based on agreed evaluation of the worth, which is converted into amounts and volumes. Such deals are still conducted, primarily between countries, and are called barter deals. When barter deals got complicated and too many items were exchanged between too many people, somehow, the counts got lost and created havoc in the market. The government of the time in Mesopotamia (modern-day Iraq) intervened and organized the deals by establishing a central registry. The registry recorded the items and their amounts and volumes based on the agreed equivalent of barley as the base measure. Thereafter, the people conducted their deals at the registry center through a registrar, who allowed the parties to receive and deliver the goods on the spot. As time went by, the deals faced a new challenge: the exchange of goods could not be made on the spot. One party needed a good that was in possession of a second party and could deliver the requested exchange on the spot, but the second party did not have the good the first party wanted for the exchange to take place but could deliver it sometime in the future. If the second party agreed, the registrar would issue a note to the effect on a clay tablet (see the photo below).

First recorded official trade deal:

A Clay Board
- Mesopotamia

Emile - Mira will pay 330 standard of barley for this plate holder at harvest time

THE FIRST CREDIT NOTE

This clay tablet is from the second millennium BC (more than four thousand years old), was inscribed in Mesopotamia, and states that Amil-Mirra will pay 330 measures of barley to the bearer of the tablet at harvest time. Note that the name of the second party is not mentioned on the tablet. That allowed the second party to use the tablet for other deals with a third party or even more parties. This was the seed idea for the inception of modern currencies. More people collected more tablets, until the registry became cumbersome for all parties.

Then, 2,700 years ago (in 700 BC), the first coin was minted in the kingdom of Lydia (modern-day Turkey). The coins were made of a combination of gold and silver known as electrum. Each coin had a standard weight that was commensurate to a standard weight or volume of barley. Coins were easier and more convenient to accumulate than tablets and were accepted for a long time—nearly 1,400 years—as the stand-alone medium of exchange. A thousand years ago (in the eleventh century), in China, during the Song dynasty, they ran out of metals and resorted to printing notes, which took five hundred years to reach Europe.

The original exchange of commodities still exists, and the banking and finance world is still working on the two original principles: give and take, or deliver and receive, or deposit and withdraw. In between the two acts, there is, as you may know, a world of types of deals, transactions, and methods of registry. Today we have virtual money, which speeds up transactions but remains as promissory as the original barter deals in prehistoric eras. The currencies you deal with, such as dollars, yuan, yen, rubles, dinars, dirhems, euros, and many more, are, in effect, barley and work the same way. If you like, we can call them barley currencies. Now imagine what you own—cash money, properties, stock shares, jewelry, cars, and other items of value—as barley. You store the barley in a silo, but you use some for your own individual needs. Then you acquire more barley, from whichever means you use.

The silo fills up, but you have more to store, so you build a larger silo or more silos and so on. The silo is your bank account. Deep inside you, you realize that only a tiny amount of the barley you have in the silo is sufficient for you for all the years you'll live and more. The amount of barley you hold in the silo can never be consumed by you in any way imaginable in this world. So why do you hold so much barley in the silo? That is, your bank account or your properties' title deeds.

I have a close friend who owns nearly $140 million. Some of it he inherited, and a good deal of it he made through his toil and wit. He goes to sleep late every night because he needs to watch the performance of the stock markets in other parts of the world with time differences between six hours, as in Hong Kong, and eleven hours, as in San Francisco. He goes to his office every morning on time and starts filling the silo. He has built many silos but always looks at the most recently built silo, which is always not fully filled. He goes around like a hungry, wild tiger, disseminating anger, fear, anxiety, tension, instability, and grudges in the work environment and among others. One night I saw him at a friend's house, and he was apprehensive, depressed, and ill at ease. I asked him what was annoying him. He was unable to pinpoint anything specific that could have led to any real cause that could be released. We talked for a long time, during which I tried to help him become aware of himself and slowly draw him into the present time as a prerequisite. He asked me to meet him again soon, so I did.

That day, we went for a long walk on a public beach. All the way, which took us three hours, including occasional breaks for drinks, I tried to let him talk. As I listened, surprisingly, he looked at me and said, "What I am going through is not worth it, is it?"

In return, I asked him, "Is what you are going through real, to be worth it or not?"

I tried to explain to him that nothing real in this world can be threatening and causing him misery, and nothing unreal exists to cause him so much apprehension and pain. He obviously possessed a strong ego that was tapping into his massive pain bodies, which he was unaware of. At the end of our walk, he asked me if he should quit his business and retire. I suggested the contrary: he should do everything he was doing, and he needed to change only his mindset, perception, and awareness. The problem was not in his business or his silos. These, like other resources, are neutral and can be employed for good purposes and for the good of the people. It was not easy for him to grasp what I was saying. I was aware that if he decided to retire, his ego would follow him and use other triggers that would bring him back to the same situation only to say, "Now what?"

My friend was strongly egoic, deeply narcissistic, and highly irrational but full of wit and vigor that made him succeed in most of his endeavors. As you may see, his problem was not external but his attachment to the external. He was a type whose ego made an image of a poor man out of him and made it live in his mind all the time. He became a poor man despite the fact that he owned $140 million. He would never become rich in his situation, even if he owned the whole world. You will understand his case more as I provide more explanation below in the general context of the lure of money.

THE LURE OF MONEY

For many people, accumulating wealth, and getting fame out of it, gives them a surge of egoic energy and motivation to follow. These people would not be attracted to any notion that calls for inner self-transcendence and mind awareness or to the divine purpose of life and would consider them baloney and obsolete. But in the long run, these people collide with the reality of a broader sense of existence, the sphere beyond the physical realm.

Such people often take up jobs or fields that can gain them the maximum amount of wealth and the widest exposure. Their focus is on the growth of their wealth, with no attention to job satisfaction or fulfillment of their natural talents. The fields they select usually are full of people of the same profile, and they all jostle with one another, as the rivalry is fierce. They all could be witty and full of vigor that makes them successful in their pursuits, but inevitably, they start to burn out, become restless, and lose interest in the job. They go on seeking different ways of making wealth and receiving recognition. Due to the fact that they are somewhat disconnected from reality and shortsighted, they tend to make crushing mistakes and lose a sizeable part of their wealth and image.

Wealth and fame that last come from genuine pursuits of originality and fullness, rather than from mimicking the paths of others. If we make wealth and fame our main aims in life, we will never really realize our talents and potential, which are the natural sources of our joy and pleasure.

What usually encourages people to run solely after wealth and exposure is their need to compare themselves to others, have more than others, and feel superior to others. With this aim in mind, they never know when to stop, or they cannot ever stop, because there are always others who rank above them, and they are too many. Eventually, they get obsessed, depressed, and disoriented, and they may lose what they have made.

JOURNEY AND DESTINATION

You always attain more if you don't obsessively chase what you want to attain. We all know that when we want to do something and give excessive attention, we usually become overanxious about the result and make a mess of it. If you want more wealth and fame, focus on the core process of your activity, and excel in it. Making more wealth and having more fame are not results of anything valuable; they are by-products. Most of the joyful moments we have are the results of genuine toil and dedication. When genuinely successful people were asked how they made huge wealth and received so much fame, at times in a relatively short time, they always said wealth and fame were not the main aims of their focus. They had a high sense of purpose of producing or offering the best possible for the good of others, which amassed huge wealth and wide exposure they never needed or used for personal gratification.

Being entangled by the complexity and time-consuming intricacies of the means, a way of never-ending lure of external forms. When the destiny is to unite with the divine self, the external forms are no more than a ladder that takes you higher, but if you stay on the ladder because you are deluded by the few steps, you will stay on the ladder for too long. You may enjoy the short height, but this height is only tying you to more vices than virtues. Rumi said the following:

> Within a Human being is such a love, a passion, and longing, an itch, a desire, that, even if he were to possess a hundred thousand worlds, he would still not find rest or peace.
>
> People try their hand at all sorts of trades and professions—they learn astronomy and medicine and so forth—but they are not at peace because they have not found what they are seeking, because the heart finds tranquillity through the beloved, so how can it find tranquillity through anything else?
>
> All these pleasures and objects of search are like a ladder. Ladder rungs are not places to stay and abide, but rather are to pass through.
>
> The sooner one awakens and becomes aware and watchful, the shorter the road becomes and the less one's life is wasted on these "ladder rungs."

DETACHMENT

I left my wealthy friend with popular sayings by Schucman:

> Nothing real can be threatened.
> Nothing unreal exists.
> Here is the peace of God.

He eventually realized he needed to become real so he could not be threatened.

It was necessary to start the journey of realization without quitting his job, for two reasons. First, realization in challenging life situations produces a stronger and more sustainable lift. Second, his job was producing good results for society—he employed seven hundred people—and contributed to the growth of the economy. He will, hopefully, reach a level of awareness where he will evaluate his personal life. He already voiced it to me during our beach walk: "It is not worth it, is it?" Sooner or later, he will answer himself.

Detachment is a process of living a normal life and possessing things and wealth and enjoying them without seeking value and identity from them. When you reach this level of consciousness, you normally say, "This is the car I drive," not "This is my car," or "I live in this house," not "This is my house," or "My job is engineer," not "I am an engineer," and so forth. It is necessary to detach yourself from your belongings and identities because you may enjoy them for your comfort and convenience while you have them, but nothing happens to you if you lose any one or even all of them, as might happen during crises or natural disasters or the down cycle of life. You may have seen people on TV come out of natural disasters having lost their houses and belongings. Some look at the ruins of their houses with smiles on their faces, saying, "We will build it again, but for now, we must find a temporary place to live." Others scream, shout, and condemn their fate, claiming that is the end of their lives. Both have experienced the same losses and dispositions. Both eventually will resettle. "This too shall pass" applies for both of them. But one will do so with serenity, and the other will do so with pain, maybe for the rest of his or her life. The first was detached from his or her possessions; the other was intensely identified with them, and he or she felt lost himself or herself. A middle-aged lady once appeared on the TV news and, while looking at the ruins of her house, said, "I am lost. I am nothing now."

Life situations will, inescapably but necessarily, appear in our lives with varying intensities to confront us with challenges and pains so that hopefully, we become more aware and more conscious. We should not expect life to be at our service. That certainly will not make you happy.

Life gives the exact doses of challenges to bring out what is already in you. Rumi said, "I did not come to add anything new to you, just came to bring out a beauty, you did not know existed in you."

FAILURE SUCCESS

A friend of mine who came from a modest background and had basic education managed, through persistence and clear vision, to become a successful banker. He earned a high salary and also earned lucrative returns from his private investments he did on the side. His wealth grew so much that he could buy properties in prime areas of a few European capitals. He was kind, helped many people, provided a luxurious living style for his family, and was a well-read and cultured person. He went on attracting success after success, until one day the proceedings started signaling that things were turning on him. Day after day, the situation got out of his hands. He lost his job, and his private investments went astray. With much support from friends, he could not pick up in any slight way. He was officially declared bankrupt and started living on Social Security benefits. At that time, for the first time, I realized he had strong pain bodies from his childhood, and his ego received him in his worst condition. Depression invaded him, his anxiety rose, his temper flared, and that led his family into a state of instability and insecurities. His health started deteriorating, first with high blood pressure and then a minor heart attack, and his weight crumbled. He lived miserably for six years, until he encountered a massive heart attack and died imminently.

To save his career and his life, my friend needed a glimpse of consciousness—the realization "This too shall pass"—and needed to re-collect his life. But his ego was viciously present and pulled the strongest and most dormant of his pain bodies, which made him suffer intensely and surrounded him painstakingly, to never look for reinstatement. One moment of awareness could have saved a diligent, useful person.

SUCCESSFUL FAILURE

In contrast to my friend's case is the case of Soichiro Honda. His case is mentioned in a little book entitled *Notes from a Friend* by Anthony Robbins, an American author, coach, and speaker.

In 1938, Honda was a poor student who had a dream of designing a piston ring to manufacture and sell to the Toyota Corporation. Every day he would go to school in the morning, and at night, all night, he would work on his design. He spent the little money he had and then sold his wife's jewelry to continue his work. After years of trial-and-error work, he managed to finalize the design and was sure Toyota would buy it. Toyota rejected it outright. Honda returned to school to face humiliation by his teachers and fellow students and shame for his failure. He was obviously disappointed, annoyed, and broke. But he was vigorously determined to continue. For the next two years, he toiled ceaselessly, until finally, he made a design Toyota bought.

To build his piston factory, Honda needed building materials, because the Japanese government was engaged in World War II, so none were available. It seemed he came to a dead end, but he was adamant to continue his pursuit. Quitting was not an option for him. So with his friends, he tried many ways to get the building materials he needed, and finally, he built his factory and started producing the piston ring.

During the war, American fighter jets bombed Honda's factory, destroying most of it. You may think Honda was devastated; instead, he asked his employees to go to where the planes dropped their fuel cans, which contained materials Honda needed for the manufacturing process that were not available anywhere in Japan. Finally, an earthquake ruined his factory, and he had no option but to sell his piston operation to Toyota. When the war ended, Japan was in a devastating condition. Resources of all kinds were scarce. Fuel was rationed and, in some cases, was almost impossible to find. Honda was unable to find enough fuel to drive his car to buy food for his family. Instead of retreating, he noticed a little motor he had that was the size and type to drive a traditional lawn mower, and he got the idea to hook it up to his bicycle. In that moment, the first motorized bike was created. He drove it for his commuting, and soon after, his friends asked him to make some for them. He made so many motorbikes that he ran out of motors, and eventually, he decided to build a new factory to manufacture complete motorbikes of his own. But he had no finances, and Japan had nothing to offer. Again, he would not surrender. He decided to write to every single bicycle shop owner in Japan, telling them he had the solution to keep the country moving and promising that his motorbike would be affordable. Then he asked them to invest in his new project.

Of the eighteen thousand bicycle shops Honda wrote to, three thousand agreed to invest in the project. He faced yet another hurdle: the motorbike was too big and bulky, and few Japanese bought it. Honda again determined to go over it. He modified the design and made it much lighter and smaller. He called it the Cub, and it became an imminent success, winning Honda the Emperor's Award.

Today Honda Corporation employs more than one hundred thousand people and outsells all but Toyota cars in the United States.

AWARENESS OF ADVERSITIES

Adversities, experiences, and life situations inevitably come to us, and at times, due to our perception of life, we invite them. People react differently to the challenges of life. Some are aware that the challenges go through them and eventually vanish, delivering triumphs and growth. Others are unaware and let the ego convince them that the challenges are of them and meant to stay, which eventually brings misery and devastation to their lives.

Two different cases mentioned earlier were the absolute manifestation of the right perception of life and the ego-induced perception of it. Honda kept himself highly aware that he was a mere receiver of the adversities, and through the process of acceptance, he was also aware of the reality that he had a duty as an individual to deal with challenges that would, later on, lead him to higher consciousness and better abilities to achieve more and better. Honda would not allow adversities to stay with him longer than necessary and would not allow them to harm, stain, or disturb him. Honda knew that adversities in all forms and shapes came and went through himself and others. We are all mediums of reception, like TV sets. A TV set receives all sorts of life experiences and situations through news programs, movies, documentaries, and so forth. Honda, as a TV set, was aware that whatever appeared on the screen was fleeting. Good or bad, sad or happy, it would travel through the screen and disappear. None of these appearing and vanishing images of objects have the power to damage the TV set and, in particular, the screen. The screen is your awareness that knows things are happening and keeps watching them, knowing they are created not by the TV set but by some external broadcasters—in your case, your ego transmitting your pain bodies and memories onto your screen. When you are able to separate yourself from the content of the screen, you will get on with life more skillfully and joyfully.

Sadly, in the case of my banker friend, he was intensely unaware, and his ego—his broadcaster—convinced him to identify himself with the content of his screen and to believe it was going to stay with him. When you cannot separate yourself from the content of life situations and you accept that they are going to linger with you for the rest of your life, you are condemned to either live in misery and pain or end your life, as happened with my banker friend.

The awareness is always independent of your perception of your experiences. It can accommodate them but cannot be influenced by them. They come and go, but your awareness stays intact. Your awareness is essential to your experiences of your life situations, but the converse is not true. Your experiences of your life situations are not essential to the vastness of your awareness. The sky is essential to the cloud, but the cloud is not essential to the sky. Clouds come and go, but the sky stays vast and expanding. The space of your awareness is always independent of the events happening in it. Events come and go, but the space stays as it is. If you are in a room with other people, whether you are fighting or dancing, the space in the room will always be the same. When you leave the room, the space in the room will be there to accommodate another life situation, happy or sad, painful or joyful. You are the sky, and your life challenges are fleeting clouds.

CHAPTER 13

LIFE BETRAYALS

THE BATTLEFIELD

THE OBJECTIVE EXPERIENCES OF LIFE have failed to help us reach our innate abilities of experiencing the peace, happiness, love, purity, wisdom, power, and knowledge we have been gifted by the divine. We, as individuals and as groups, have allowed our egos to play vicious games with us and among us. The world we live in has turned into a battlefield we need to enter every day. Everywhere you meet people is a battlefield. The workplace, the home, schools, the marketplace, roads, and even spiritual places are all battlefields. If you think differently, you are risking your existence. When you go out into the world, you necessarily need to be aware that you're entering a battlefield. You need to soften on moralizing and idealizing the world. We all know we need to be good, loving, caring, and accommodating, but entering a battlefield with a flower bouquet will expose you to many risks of abuse, misuse, lies, treacheries, plunder, floggings, and more. In no way, on your part, should you inflict them on others. But in a practical and realistic sense, you should not go out presenting flowers to the offending adversaries. The least you can do is to protect yourself against their offenses. Take a protective shield with you. This shield is your awareness of people's nature and behaviors, most of which are hidden under their masks. Some masks are thicker than others.

In the earlier chapters, I explained the natures and behaviors of people in a wider sense; here I will reveal more with some in-depth details and shrewdness.

The realities of life that you will read hereunder do not suggest any judgments. They are not right or wrong. They are as they are seen and need to be dealt with in a realistic manner. In becoming more realistic, you are simply becoming more conscious.

FIFTY WAYS TO KNOW PEOPLE

1. The most superior people are innately as superior as you are. What makes people superior is their level of awareness and nothing else.
2. People never show their real faces or intentions. They always wear masks, and they disguise the truth most of the time. Power and money do not corrupt people; they just reveal what was hidden behind their masks.
3. Those who show power and authority do not have them. Deep in their inner selves lie intense fear, a sense of insecurity, and inferiority.
4. Some people look nice, polite, caring, and charismatic until they do not need to be; then their vicious realities will pour out.
5. So-called successful people need a lot of attention. Do not give it to them, because they will start harming you to give them more attention. There is no limit to their need for attention. Real successful people do not know they are successful, and when they are told, they do not pay attention.
6. People who call for morality are lured to immorality deep inside. They call for forbidding immorality repeatedly because the lure of immorality is always in their minds.
7. People mostly harm not when they are hungry but when they are full. That is why, when people become overabundant, they exploit more and loot more. They think it is their acquired right; hence, they do not feel guilty.
8. People who strive to help you will milk you later.
9. People who partner with each other are mostly out to hunt each other. *Partnership* is a romantic name for hunting.

10. People marry only for vested interest and convenience. The rest are sugarcoating, which will melt sooner rather than later.

11. The closer people get to their goals, the more they become prone to discontent and frustration with their affairs. Their joy stems from the process of achieving, rather than from achieving the goal.

12. People do not necessarily want freedom, because with it come the weight of responsibility and accompanying frustration.

13. Extremist people fear freedom more than oppression.

14. Most people risk for what they do not need more than for their actual needs.

15. People favor equality without freedom more than freedom without equality.

16. People with the loudest voices for freedom are those who are less happy in a free society or environment.

17. People who show off prosperity and selfishness are strongly prone to depression and self-pity.

18. People who scarifice their time and energy with strong convictions are those who have been disconnected from their inner real selves. They do not know who they are, so they do not mind destroying themselves in the name of charity, humanity, democracy, or God.

19. People strongly and blindly believe in subjects they do not understand. The more ambiguous the subjects are, the stronger and longer their convictions are.

20. People who show off modesty are those who yearn for the items they claim they dispense of.

21. The merchant, executive, financier, social activist, political activist, and religious preacher hunt their prey in the same forest, the forest of hopelessness and misery.

22. There has not been one merciful nation in the entire history of mankind. People usually follow their history.

23. People like to imitate others as much as they dislike themselves and want to sever ties with themselves.

24. People like to imitate those who are different from them, rather than those who are the same.

25. People mostly want to follow a leader or a boss, not so he will lead them somewhere but so he will lead them anywhere away from themselves, whom they loathe.

26. People who are ready to follow blindly and work with absolute loyalty are those who want to disconnect from themselves.

27. People who feel comfortable following strict rules, regulations, and work regimes are those who want to miss their individuality and paralyze their minds.

28. People in groups who repeat chants, slogans, songs, verses, and rituals, no matter where they chant, become stringent and obstinate.

29. People who seek to find flaws in others are those who suffer the same flaws.

30. People are prepared to go to the furthest extent only when they do not know where they are going.

31. People who experience a difficulty that prevents them from carrying out their duties, even if it is a medical condition, turn to change the world for their purpose.

32. People who cannot claim mastery for themselves find it convenient to claim it for their work group, their nation, their race, their religion, or any sacred cause. These people will go where they cannot see themselves.

33. People who extend their hands to pull out others, in fact, are looking for hands to pull them away.

34. People feel more frustrated when they have plenty and want more—more than when they have nothing and want little.

35. People are less frustrated when they lose a lot than when they lose one thing.

36. People of authority at work who want to exploit the workers to their maximum output usually seek to create division among the workers and turn individuals against one another. Always, you see them fail in their quest.

37. People of authority at work who demonstrate excessive power and control are usually selfish, fearful, and incompetent and are forced by their egos to utilize their flaws against subordinates and others in the name of work commitment.

38. People become more frustrated when they face unlimited opportunities than when they have limited or no opportunities.

39. People deny their responsibilities and duties of the present time when they are promised future gains. The stronger the promises are, the more they disregard and even hate the present time, which may lead them to work against the current affairs.

40. People pray not only for their daily bread but also for their daily illusions.

41. People most receptive to media content, particularly advertisements and propaganda, are usually those who have lost hope in themselves and are frustrated.

42. People who are not productive or not successful usually are those who want to scarifice what they do not have by pulling what others have. These are the people seen in campaigns for collecting for charities and calling for reforms.

43. Super intelligence and nubilous character are seen as unessential and even unfavored by many people.

44. The most and least successful people tend to be similarly frustrated and depressed. Both look at you as their source of pain and treat you accordingly.

45. The face value of people's talk is always less than its real value.

46. People who walk behind you are always more dangerous than those who walk in front of you.

47. People are mostly drawn toward negative biases and what is wrong, not what is right. Complaining and griping are their two main expressions.

48. People volunteer to offer you advice and support exactly when you do not need them. They make you indebted to them without any cost to themselves.

49. People come in all varieties, like fruits or stones: foolish, saintly, sociopathic, egomaniacal, sensitive, insensitive, noble, ruthless, and so forth. They are as they are and will remain so, at least for the realizable period. You can deal with all varieties when you keep your awareness high and present.

THE INNER ENERGY FIELD: THE INWARD JOURNEY

If the ego runs your mind, your life is run by it. Ego-run life is treacherous, confusing, and trapping. You cannot be at rest at any time in ego's presence in your mind, nor can you be fulfilled in any way, except for during short periods when the ego gives you sedative doses of false relief when you obtain what it has suggested to you and when your induced want has just been met. Since the ego is a false self, it cannot feed on your inner-self substances; it goes to identify with the external forms and calls to be fed and defended as long as you are unaware and, hence, obedient. The most common ego-identification needs are derived not from you but from your possessions, family background, education, knowledge, status, appearance, abilities, networks, race, religion, and other collective identities. All of these are accessories of your life and bear no essence in your true self.

We all strive to disconnect the ego from the mind. This is incorrect. We need to reconnect the inner self, or the inner body or the source, with the mind. We need to reach to this source, which is unmanifested for most of our lives. In our sleep, particularly our deep sleep, we touch this zone and draw vital energy from it, until we wake up and return to the physical domain of the manifested world of separate accessories. This journey in a deep-sleep state is involuntary, and you do not exist in that state. Our main goal in life is to reach that state when we are awake.

In your wakeful life, you cannot access the unmanifested unless you are conscious. This means only in the absence of the ego. The unmanifested will not come to liberate you from the ego. In the Arabic language, it is called *Alhaq*—the Truth. This is not the truth that people search for outside themselves in mosques, churches, and ashrams or elsewhere. These places can only offer you the conceptual truth or even part of it, as most rituals are performed at physical and perceptual levels. You may go into a hypnotic state in which you try to dream while awake, but it does not get you to the unmanifested, the Alhaq. It does not free you from the ego, but it may give you brief periods of trance and fascination.

JOURNEY TO THE UNMANIFESTED: ALHAQ

The journey to the Alhaq, the unmanifested, is inward, through the inner energy field of the body. This field is a path you can only step into by entering the body. Implicitly, you cannot enter your body by being or entering somewhere else. You cannot enter your body if your mind is engaging you in the past or the future. You need to be in the here and now, present in the now. That is the doorstep of the entry of your body. Here time dissolves, your mind halts, and your ego is disabled and made powerless. This is also called *present-moment awareness*, when you become conscious of the unmanifested. Becoming intensely present, as a direct one-step-ritual fast track, is accessible to ascetic and yogi devotees, who can shift from the form to the formless in a relatively short time. For the majority, it is best attained first through conscious breathing and then through sense perception of observation, listening to, touching, and smelling the forms in nature or living species, coupled with being in a state of intense awareness. This way, your mind will stop running commentary. You do not need to force your mind to stop thinking. As you enter the formless, the mind has no room to function, as it belongs to the manifested realm, and the incessant thought will gradually fade away. This is meditation in its exact practical functioning. In this meditative state, you start becoming conscious of the unmanifested—conscious of the formless and timeless divine essence in your inner self and in all species, creatures, and nature.

ACCEPT WHAT IS

Being in a meditative state helps you to observe the nature of the thoughts the ego has engrained in your mind for so long and to attempt to reverse or revoke them through realization and acceptance of what is. This is another way to enter the gateway to the energy field of the unmanifested. When you do not accept what is, you increase your inner resistance that cuts you off from your real self, people, and the world around you. The ego will strengthen the feeling of separateness, on which it thrives. The more you feel you are separated, the more you will manifest the world of forms and be influenced by external events, and it becomes harder to be aware of the reality of life. The gateway is closed, and you are cut off from the inner self, the source. When you realize and accept what is, your form identity dilutes and dissolves, allowing the unmanifested to permeate through you. As soon as the gateway opens and you reach the energy field of your inner source, all seven divine components will emerge in your being: peace, happiness, love, purity, knowledge, wisdom, and power.

SOUND OF SILENCE

Along with conscious breathing, sense perception, and acceptance, the gateway of silence is another dimension that helps you to access your inner energy field. The world is filled more with silence than with sounds. Listening to the silence, you hear the voice of nothingness, which is the voice of your inner self, the sound of the unmanifested. The ego has, through its incessant urge, taught us that hearing is for listening to the manifested source, which is external. When you listen to the silence, the universe, through your etheric layer into your inner self, bestows on you talk that cannot ever be communicated to you in any way by any other source.

Prophet Muhammad (PBUH) regularly went up Alnoor Mountain in Mecca and stayed in seclusion in Alhurra laurel for extended periods, listening to the silence, until one day, a soundless voice descended on him and told him, "Recite."

Prophet Muhammad (PBUH), who was an illiterate man, replied, "I am not a reciter."

Then the voice said the following:

> Recite in the name of your Lord who created,
> Created man from the clots of blood,
> Recite, your Lord is the Most Bountiful one. (Alalaq 113:1–3)
> This was the dawn of Islam, which is now followed by two billion people and is the fastest-growing religion in the world.
> The voice was the voice of silence, the voice of God.
> If you want to listen to God, listen to the voice of silence.

Pay attention to the silence—in your room, in between sentences. The more you listen to the silence, the more you become still within. The silence in the external world induces stillness in the inner self, where you enter the unmanifested.

NOTHINGNESS

Sound cannot exist unless there is silence, as things cannot exist without space—nothingness—that can hold them. Every physical form was born out of nothing and laid in nothing and will return to nothing. The world we live in is formed of nothing. The universe at large is nothing. Every solid object is a bundle of vibrating empty atoms. Your physical body is 99.99 percent empty space.

The world around you is space with solidified vibrating physical forms, illusioned to you by your perception and experience as things, as manifested forms. The unmanifested is not only ever-present in your inner self but also connected to the world and the wider consciousness that pervades the entire universe as nothingness and silence. Both nothingness and silence remain independent, constant, and neutral, no matter what your mind perceives anywhere, in any way, and at any time. Paying attention to nothingness—space—and silence opens the gateway for us to realize the unmanifested, which is the main purpose of our existence.

STILLNESS

Together nothingness and silence induce stillness, which forms the breeding ground for ever-expanding consciousness of all existence. Although they do not have existence, they enable everything else to exist. You cannot sense silence, but in silence, you sense and hear talk, music, noise, and other sounds. Equally, you cannot touch space, but in space, you can see and touch furniture, a TV set, curtains, windows, walls, paintings, and so on.

The sounds you hear in the silence are not of the silence, and the furniture in the room is not the room. When either or both are not paid attention to, you miss both. When you do, a shift in consciousness takes place in you. As with conscious breathing and sense perception, being aware of space and silence will stop you from thinking at the same time. The space and silence imply nothingness—space of no mind, of pure consciousness, and, ultimately, of the unmanifested. The space and silence, being nothing, do not exist. Only when sound appears do you realize the silence, and only when furniture or any physical objects are put in the room space do you realize the space. This realization raises your awareness and beingness, which leads you to appreciate, value, love, and respect not only the inner-self values but also the physical items that appear in the space and silence, such as furniture, music, and other things. You also will realize that all these things will eventually dissolve and do not matter that much. At this juncture, you have overtaken the world for peace and happiness.

CHAPTER 14

THE MADNESS OF THE WORLD

OPTIMISM AND PRAGMATISM

THE WORLD IS NOT A place for much joy and pleasure. It is shaped for things to go wrong, and seldom do things go right. When something does go right, we call it luck, fortune, or even a miracle. We innately know this reality and, to some extent, covertly, like it, but we go astray when things go wrong for us personally. We like the thrill of things going wrong for others and elsewhere, and we like it more when things go disastrously and when people inflict injuries upon each other. You may deny this fact. But you pay money to watch movies based on things going wrong. Someone is killed, couples separate, houses burn down, war leaves devastation, ships sink, planes crash, and hurricanes and earthquakes hit. Even sports programs show you who has lost and been demeaned and so on. If these movies and programs showed happy episodes, most people would not watch them, never mind pay for them; the movie industry would collapse, and the sports industry would disintegrate in a short span of time.

The world is not going to revamp anytime in the future that we can imagine; no savior is on the way, as much as we prophesize. However, as individuals, we can contribute toward making the world better for all of humanity. We can take more effective strides, first and foremost by being realistic that the world is in a rigid state that has been formed over at least five billion years and that humanity has been malfunctioning for more than eighty thousand years and has encumbered the lives of thousands of generations with legacies of atrocities, savagery, and irrationalities.

We all need doses of optimism, with stronger doses of caution and pragmatism.

EMPTYING THE OCEAN WITH A SPOON

Greek philosophers were highly insightful and brilliant in their fields. Aristotle was told by Heraclitus, another Greek philosopher, to avoid extending his logic to every aspect of life with thoughts. Heraclitus explained to Aristotle that what he was doing was emptying the ocean into a hole with a spoon.

The ocean was divine knowledge, the hole was the human mind, and the spoon was Aristotle's ability to deliver.

There are many spiritual schools, many religions, and many approaches that attempt to help people to awaken and elevate their consciousness for better insight into their inner-self treasures of life. A sizeable number of these have turned into Aristotelian delusion and converted spirituality into rituality, progressing as entertaining entities. Others have turned into money-collecting depots and largely derailed into compromising conditions and egoic behaviors. A minority remain original, genuine, and highly impactful.

Be cautious not to be driven into emptying the ocean with a spoon. To enhance your awareness and your consciousness, you need not resort to deep conviction or deep yogi practices. Both require strong devotion that eventually leads to delusion and stagnation, which may result in some sort of fanaticism against self or others. One is self-immersion; the other is self-rejection. No one needs either. What you need in physical exercise is to keep your body fit for your normal daily life. Going to sports centers for heavy weightlifting will build your muscles to a monumental scale you do not know what to do with and cannot use in your normal daily life, and you may end up harming your health or end up participating in bodybuilder shows, feeding your ego. Recently, I a saw a heavyweight bodybuilder working at a reception desk.

When your body needs more strength, it has intelligence that captures your requirement and builds itself to your requirement. Even the skin of your palms gets coarse when you start manual activities.

BALANCE OF HUMAN AND BEING

The practice of awareness and consciousness is like your normal daily physical fitness exercise; it should be related to your normal daily life. Deep conviction and deep yogi practices in any school or teaching are like heavyweight bodybuilding; you do not know what to do with the muscles and may harm yourself and possibly others. Self-immersion and self-rejection are both sides of your purpose in life. We need, in normal life situations, to balance between the human side and the being side. The best is, of course, staying in the being role while performing your human functions. Here, if the devotion is on both sides, it works at its most constructive role.

Sadhguru, in his book *Inner Engineering*, talks about an intense yogi—or, as he calls him, legendary yogi—from southern India. His name was Sadashiva Brahmendra. He was called a *nirkaya*, which literally means "bodiless yogi." He walked around naked and had no sense of home, property, or physical boundaries.

One day he happened to walk into the king's garden. The king was sitting there, relaxing with his queens. Brahmendra wandered into the garden, unaware of his nakedness. The king was furious and sent soldiers after him. The soldiers ran after Brahmendra, calling out to him. He did not turn back and continued his walk. Angered, one of the soldiers took out his sword and struck, severing Brahmendra's right arm. Brahmendra continued his walk without even breaking his stride.

The soldiers were wonderstruck and terrified. They realized Brahmendra was no ordinary man. The king and his soldiers ran after him, prostrated, begged his forgiveness, and brought him back to the garden for the rest of his life.

When the energy field of the inner self is heightened, the sense of the physical is diminished. That makes it possible to go without food for many days.

Brahmendra was intensely in the being state, but we know nothing about his human side. What did his intense being offer the external world, the world where the universe passes its purpose through human beings?

Imam Ali (PBUH), the son-in-law of Prophet Muhammad, was the fourth caliph of Islam after Prophet Muhammad (PBUH). During his rule, a rival family called Bani Umaia claimed the reign of the state of Islam. Imam Ali (PBUH) was assassinated on behalf of the Bani Umaia by Abdul Rahman Ibn Muljam, who struck a sword on Imam Ali's skull while he was performing his prayers in a mosque. Imam Ali (PBUH) continued his prayers for some time without realizing he had been struck, until he completed his prayers and moved up.

When Imam Ali (PBUH) was struck, he was in an intense being state. His inner energy field was so high that the sense of his physical body diminished fully. He would pray in that state five times every day.

After his prayer, Iman Ali (PBUH) would attend to his duties as caliph of Islam, do farming for his food, and write literature on philosophy and the rule of justice. His book *Nahej Albalagha* is a living book and widely valued even by many non-Muslims.

Imam Ali (PBUH) attended to both parts of his life. His being part was highly intense, and his human part was extensive. He blended the two, which served humanity in its best form, leaving a revered legacy manifesting great human consciousness. That was his awakened doing.

AWARENESS OF CHALLENGES

You may occasionally go to schools, ashrams, temples, or prayer places and watch videos or read books to learn more skills and practices as a seeker, not as a devotee. It is essential that you practice what you learn in your normal daily activities and environment—at traffic lights, in the fish market, at work, at home, when meeting difficult people. These teachings are meant for these places. In temples, ashrams, prayer places, and others, you normally have a nice and peaceful ambience, and the people there are nice and kind. What you seek when you go there is already in you. The ambience and teachers act as triggers to help you unveil it. We must never expect that in these places are things you can acquire.

It is essential that what you learn you practice at the human level.

Retreating in prayer places, temples, and mountaintops is useful and necessary but to the limit that allows us to go back to the world to honor our divine duties.

Rabindranath Tagore was a great Indian thinker and was best known as a poet and philosopher. He was the first non-European writer to be awarded the Nobel Prize, in 1913 for literature.

Tagore, in one of his writings, talked to a monk in a temple:

> Whom do you worship in that dark corner of the temple? All windows of which are closed.
>
> Open your eyes and look, to see, that God is not in front of you, here.
>
> The God is there, where the farmer plows the coarse earth.
>
> And along the way where the worker toils to break the stones, in his dusty clothes.
>
> The God is there with them, under the burning sun and hail rain. Take off your coat and land on the earth to meet them and God. Leave your reflections and let your flowers and your incense. What harm if your clothes are torn or dirtied? Go and be, beside God, toiling and sweating.

THE CYCLIC MOTION OF LIFE

The world around us has its own cyclic rhythm, which is part of the wider universal coming-and-going, not necessarily changing, as we might believe. Some of these cyclic movements are very short, such as the inhalation and exhalation of your breath, as well as expansion and contraction of your heart. This is also reflected in the cycle of sleep and wakefulness, which is the cycle of going between the manifested and the unmanifested.

The coming-and-going cycle is also reflected in the lives of individuals. We come to this world, we grow both physically and mentally, then we start decaying, and finally, we go. The same applies to the rise and fall of nations, cultures, and civilizations.

IBN KHALDUN: GENERATIONAL CYCLES

The great fourteenth-century Islamic scholar Ibn Khaldun first formulated this idea into the theory that history seems to move in a coming-and-going cycle in four acts of four generations.

The first generation makes a radical break with the status quo, establishing new values and drives, which might seem chaotic, but also in this generation, great leaders, thinkers, and reformers appear and influence the course of the proceedings of the coming and leave their imprints.

The second generation has a better sense of direction and establishes some order. Although they are still attached to the spark of the initial coming, they drive toward stability, establishing constitutions and doctrines.

The third generation comes with less heat and passion, having little connection to the initial coming. They are more realistic and practical. They want to develop and make life more stable and comfortable. They are attracted not to the original ideas and beliefs of the first generation but, rather, to building and producing. As time passes, they extinguish the flame of the first generation. Thereafter, materialism and individualism dominate the lives of the people.

The fourth generation comes with hesitation, lack of interest, and blurred direction. They sense the problems, but they do not have solutions. They begin to doubt the values of the previous generations and even become cynical and pessimistic. Nobody knows where to stand. General discontent appears, which leads to chaos. Then the new first generation comes, which stands under a new belief and tears down the old order. The new cycle starts.

The Ibn Khaldun theory is vivid in the above cyclic coming-and-going pattern. It can be summarized as follows:

> Hard times create strong men.
> Strong men create good times.
> Good times create weak men.
> Weak men create hard times.

This pattern has some variations and is not an exact science. But we see numerous sequences of the generations, particularly the fourth generation, when crises emerge and, with them, chaos and pain.

This pattern is also applicable to elected government, heads of state, and corporations, although the cycle periods are much shorter. The cycle for ruling regimes may last for nearly a hundred years, with each generation's life span about twenty-five years. For corporations, the overall cycle takes nearly eighty years or shorter.

German socialist philosopher Karl Marx, the father of communism, said, "History repeats itself, first as a tragedy, second as a farce." Yes, it does but only if history is sailed by unconscious people. If you are conscious and intervene, you can shape history to your advantage.

As human beings, we are not condemned by this pattern as a fate. We can change the course of the cycle by intervening in the motion and by introducing innovative ideas, concepts, systems, and approaches, particularly during the second part of the second generation, before the end of the first part of the third generation, and certainly before the coming of the fourth generation and its inevitable downfall.

CORPORATE GENERATIONAL CYCLES

For corporations, every generation should intervene to induce sustainability, because corporations are much more fragile than any other entities. Their business momentum can be extinguished by the cyclic motion as fast as the second generation by a multitude of uncontrollable external variables. The major act for executives of corporations is to push the targets always higher than the previous year's achievements, defusing the potential complacency that previous successes may generate. This creates ongoing challenges. When you reach a mountaintop, aim for another higher mountaintop. The stay on any mountaintop is, by implication, short, and you must leave soon. If you do not leave upward to a higher mountaintop, you will have no choice but to drop down to a lower mountaintop. This executive intervention must be proliferated across functions and resources proportionately.

The cyclic nature of the motions, particularly the corporate motion, forces movement in an upward direction. If you are not going upward, you are condemned by the cyclic motion to slip downward. There is no stability at the top, and the stay period is short.

CYCLIC MOTION OF MANIFESTATION

At the individual level, as mentioned earlier, we are in the larger cycle of life, the cycle of birth and death, which is a fact we cannot escape. In the larger cycle of life, many cycles move certain parts of our lives in both physical and unmanifested domains. The major swing, and the most sensitive of all essentials to our existence, is between the manifested and the unmanifested realms of life.

The coming motion in an individual's life, relenting or salvation of form, whether through life's continuous experiences or some kind of losses and tragedies, albeit painful and agonizing, offers great opportunities for spiritual awakening and separation of consciousness from the form. It is a blessing in disguise, though many of us call it a curse and do not in any way accept it.

SAHARA DESERT DUST

Every year, the Bodélé Depression causes 182 million tons of dust to blow from the Sahara Desert over and across the Atlantic Ocean, where it touches some parts of the North American continent and then flies swiftly over the Central American region before it lands on the Amazon rain forest nearly five thousand kilometers away. The dust contains many minerals and nutrients essential for marine and forest life. Along the way, the dust feeds the ocean and large parts of the land with essential minerals and nutrients. Nearly twenty-seven million tons of dust reach the Amazon, fertilizing the nutrient-poor soil of the rain forest. Amazonian soil is short of phosphorus and other critical nutrients that get washed away by the basin's frequent and heavy rainfall.

The dust storm blows at least twice a year, in winter and spring, but blows many other times of the year. It plays a crucial role in holding the Amazon rain forest in balance, which, in turn, holds the climate system in balance, saving the ecology of the planet, without which life on Earth would be seriously endangered.

As the dust travels through the air, the dust particles both absorb and reflect sunlight, causing a high moisture level in the air, disturbing the air balance and causing storms and, at times, hurricanes.

The storms and hurricanes gather tremendous momentum, which gives them great physical thrust. This is necessary to give enough power to travel five thousand kilometers from the Sahara to the Amazon. But the power is so high that it destroys physical objects along the way. Unfortunately, if humans are along the way, their lives may be destroyed, causing massive losses and pain.

If you were caught in the storm or hurricane and faced losses, you would call it a curse, but if you were an environmentalist observer, you would call it a blessing. But to both of you, what would happen if the Sahara Desert stopped blowing dust?

The losses caused by the storms and hurricanes have awakened many people, including government, engineers, metrologists, and ecologists, to find, create, and invent many products and many solutions that have advanced the lives of humans and other species.

People who are caught in these life challenges, one way or another, invariably experience spiritual awakening—the coming of the awakening.

ADVERSITY FOR AWAKENING

Through aging, loss, and tragedies, spiritual awakening enters the lives of people. When the external forms collapse, the ego starts dissolving, and the inner enlightened self emerges. The going of the ego brings the coming of the self. This is the cyclic motion of consciousness, which has taken more than eighty thousand years from going to now the beginning of its coming, which is the beginning of the ego's going.

Nobody knows how long it will take to tangibly realize the coming of the consciousness or the going of the ego. It may not take another eighty thousand years, but it will not be anytime soon. Some people may resist the coming of consciousness because it means the destruction or disruption of the outer purposes and forms that have been forced on them for so long by the ego, and it is not conveniently possible to let go of them. They will start to realize that what is lost on the level of the external form is gained on the level of the inner essence.

COMING OF CONSCIOUSNESS

Although the coming of consciousness has certainly started, most people have yet to take the opportunity, because they are still trapped in the ego identification of the coming-and-going and the external level or form level. This tendency, unfortunately, hardens the grip of the ego, which means the shrinking of the inner self, rather than the opening of it. Here the ego plays trickier games, making you spend your time complaining, being fearful or angry, feeling guilty all the time, self-pitying, being immersed in many other mental or emotional agonies, getting attached to memories, and thinking about the past.

When the ego no longer has a grip on your life, your life becomes accommodating. It does not matter whether you are young or old; you become radiant with inner light and transparent to the light of the cosmos.

The coming cycle of consciousness has started. Take the opportunity to break open your awakening and intensify and culminate the awakening process.

Now that we are awakened and aware of the external forms and the need to deal with them at the time we need them, it is essential for the inner self to integrate with the outer world with a sense of clear purpose that stems from the purpose of the universe. The going here is the coming in disguise, and the ego will attempt with all its forces to defuse your quest for achieving anything that is of the inner-self spirit. In your quest to serve the universe by allowing the universe to pass its purposes through you, there comes the ego to usurp it and use it for its own purposes. The ego will push, first and foremost, to make you gauge yourself against others, as was your early childhood need, which possibly still lingers within your memories. It may well go further to tap into your unsatisfied childhood need to have more than this person or that person. The ego, now that it is threatened by your opening and awakening, will undoubtedly strengthen itself through identification with the outer movement of the lure toward having more and being better than others. The ego will ceaselessly persist. It is your purpose to allow your awareness and your vigilance to expand to disregard any ego-induced perception of the outer world.

As you enter the new consciousness, you do not need the world to confront you with tragedies and pain to be awakened anymore. It will surely do it for you if you stay outside the sphere of consciousness. It is safer and more peaceful to voluntarily choose the process of awakening, even when you have to deal with the outward cyclic motion of the growing and expanding external forms. You can still dwell between your inward coming movement, which includes stillness, being, and disidentification with the external forms, and your outward going, such as acquiring skills and knowledge through attending classes, practicing in real-life conditions, exercising, and observing your own mind-body interactions.

In the going motion, you are confronted with egoic dysfunction. Being conscious of it, you will weaken the ego's attempt to disrupt the alignment between your mental ability and the intelligence of the universe in the going sphere, and you will be better equipped to serve the purpose of your external world. Whatever action you take, the ego will create an opposing force equal in intensity in the form of disagreements, confrontations, or opposition. The stronger the ego is, the more strongly you create resistance and confront others. The way to defuse this egoic tendency is to drive your intentions with love and care for everybody and disconnect from your identities.

When you take actions to do or create, it is always necessary to take the right actions but also, more importantly, to take actions within your consciousness. This means your actions should necessarily stem from within your inner self. From there, you will create a new world. Without consciousness that induces a change in the world for the better, your actions will not introduce anything better to the world but will reintroduce or recondition what has already been created but redecorated by the ego for you.

UNDERSTANDING AND ACCEPTING

Earlier, I mentioned "This too shall pass." It meant the broader change in everything. It meant to give the king the reality of impermanence of the world and everything in it. It is, in fact, a cyclic motion that things convert to their opposites over time, or seemingly so. I say *seemingly* because what might seem to you as the opposite is actually an integral part of, or the other half of, the matter. It is a half of the same in a different place, condition, or form or with different energies. For example, if you are hard hit by low income, there will inevitably be a time when this hardship will dissolve and disappear. If you are conscious of this fact, you will, despite the discomfort or pain, accept the fact and allow it to pass and make room to receive the same or more. So float with it until it bounces up again and completes the cycle. If you resist the condition, you make it linger longer—as long as you cling to it. This is the down cycle, which is essential for the process of awakening.

The Koran reminds us and promises the following:

Have we not caused thy bosom to dilate?
And eased thee of the burden.
Which weighed down thy back.
And exalted thy fame.
But lo with hardship Goethe ease
Lo with hardship Goethe ease. (Al-Inshirah 94:1–7)

The repetition of the verse "Lo with hardship Goethe ease" not only connotes the promise of the return but confirms it.

Here is the reflection of the prosperity concealed in hardship. It works in reverse motion too. Every aspect of your life situation is subject to this cyclic back-and-forth, upward-and-downward, and outward-and-inward motion. The faster you accept the fall, the sooner the cycle completes and returns to you.

The cycles of life situations can last for a lifetime, such as the cycle of death and birth; a few years, as for failure and success; a few days, as for happiness and misery; or a few hours, as for joy and discontent.

ACCEPT CYCLIC MOTION

Many health problems are caused by resisting and fighting the cyclic motion of the experiences in the world, which are essential for rejuvenating and regenerating life energies. If you are identified with your mind-made egoic images of self and your consequent nonacceptance of the cyclic motion, you are lured toward delusions and empty desires.

If you succumb to this egoic force, you will resist every downward cycle and will not allow it to complete. Thus, your body intelligence will come like a savior to rescue you and create a health problem that forces you to relinquish your resistance and allow the process of rejuvenation and regeneration to take its course.

Whenever your egoic mind rejoices in a life condition or experience, be it wealth, status, a possession, appearances, a car, a house, or so on, you identify with it and get attached to it. It may make you joyful, proud, and possibly inflated, and you may believe it is your essence or what you want it to be.

But, as you are by now aware, everything changes in the manifested realm. The force of entropy de-energizes and degenerates whatever it tries to hold on to against the will of the cyclic motion of life. Whatever is in your hand will end or change or change position. In the manifested realm, people, with no exceptions, are destined to fail only to succeed again; all gains are bound to be lost only to be regained. This change or impermanence, as people call it, is, in fact, the process of realization and regeneration.

When you accept, you still respond and interact with whatever you encounter at the level of form, be it joy or misery, possession or loss, health or sickness, but hopefully, you will not be identified with it. These are not your essence; they are experiences you go through. They come and go like clouds, but the sky remains, like you, intact.

The two polarities of anything are, in fact, one thing separated in time. Gain and loss are the same; neither can exist without the other. They are not against each other but merely out of phase in time. When you wait and are patient, both gain and loss will pass through you, possibly a few times, in your lifetime.

YOU FIND IT WHERE YOU LOST IT

In the beginning of the book, I mentioned that humanity lost its awareness and consciousness along the way until now. Many thinkers and spiritual leaders believe it has become oblivious and irrational. Sadhguru and Robert Greene go further and call it insane.

Humanity did not lose its awareness and consciousness in caves, on mountaintops, in temples, in prayer places, or in gyms. It lost them when physical forms overwhelmed life in the workplace, in the marketplace, at home, in the field, and in normal daily life circumstances and conditions.

You can find what you have lost only in the place where you lost it. It is futile and self-defeating to look for it anywhere else.

This book is about regaining our awareness and consciousness, and all the way through, I've suggested practical realizations, understanding, tools, and practices everyone can and should use where awareness and consciousness were lost—that is, in daily life conditions. As mentioned earlier, going to mountaintops, temples, prayer places, or gyms is fine to consolidate your practices, but do not expect to find your lost items there. Your lost items are somewhere in your daily places: in your home, in your workplace, in the marketplace, at traffic lights, on the road, in your car, and in service places.

Every suggestion made so far is to be used in your real-life conditions.

The book is nearing the end. This last part will be dedicated to specific practical applications, techniques, and tools you can carry in the pocket or box of your consciousness. They are meant to jump up for you at critical times when you need them. It is essential to practice conscious breathing and sense perception always. They are the most practical and powerful tools you may use anywhere and anytime. If you need to, go back to read about and practice them again.

———— ⟲ ————

CHAPTER 15

IT IS WHAT IT IS

THE WILL OF THE UNIVERSE

THINGS HAPPEN IN THE WORLD for millions of reasons we hardly know. They are all commanded by the will of the universe to manifest its purposes through human beings, other species, and forms. At times, things happen to our favor and liking, and we call them good omens, luck, or fortune. We may go further and call the world fair, graceful, just, a good place, and so on.

When things are not to our favor and liking, which happens often, then all our perceptions of life flounder. This is the opportune time and condition for your ego to receive you and tap into your pain bodies that have been amassed in the four layers of your memory storage. Depending on the intensity of your pain body, you tend to see the world as grim, frustrating, worrying, threatening, and so on. Then you lose your ease, lightness, and peace. Your mind becomes congested, and your physical health starts to weaken, bringing certain illnesses. It may take time for this cycle to complete. But when you are aware of the reality of the cyclic nature of the world, it helps you tremendously to alleviate the negative repercussions of the adversity you are facing.

The first step into solace is to remind yourself of the cyclic motion. Things need to drop to regenerate. That is normal, but it is unfortunate— or covertly fortunate—when it crosses your path. Awakening to this fact, you attempt to accept the situation as it is. I am aware that it is uneasy at times to reach this level of awareness quickly enough, but experience has shown the repetition of the awakening will take it to the practical level sooner than you expect. It is essential to bring yourself to this level because the only other option you have is to live in pain, agony, and ill health during the entire period of downturn of the cycle.

When you practice this awakening, over time, you find yourself still facing adverse situations but with calmness, lightness, patience, acceptance, and, above all, optimism that "This too shall pass" and "It is as it is." You accept consciously and wait gracefully. Remember, this is the only positive option you have. Do not look elsewhere.

As you live through an experience with full awareness, or when you get out of it, you will find that your inner dependency on forms is fading, and your general life is enriching. People, things, and affairs you thought were essentials of your life now are attracted to you by their will, and you do not need to go after them. You decide to value and enjoy them, knowing they too have a downturn to come. Being aware of this fact, you have no fear of losing them anymore. When they are there, it is good, and when they are not there, it is fine. As with Honda!

"It is as it is" is a state of independence, acceptance, and nonresistance that takes you to the joy of beingness. If everything collapses around you, you, like Honda, will still be understanding, wakeful, and at peace.

DISCONTENTMENT

I have a friend who had a rough childhood experience. He managed to receive higher education and got a well-paid executive job at a prestigious company. He worked there for many years and saved a lot of money. He decided to take an early retirement and start his own business. His early retirement package and his savings would outlive his living time. He excelled in his business and generated sizeable financial wealth. He has made enough money to run his life at a high standard for at least another eighty-five years, even if he does not earn more money during that period.

In my country, Bahrain, we have a dual system of services for health and education: government track, where the service is excellent in general and free, and private track, where the service is not necessarily better than the government service in all cases but highly convenient and at cost. My friend always opts to use government service because it is free, but it is always crowded and may not be convenient and comfortable. Every time he visits government health facilities, he comes back bursting with anger, irritation, and discontent. One time, the wait time was ten minutes longer than the scheduled time, and another time, there was no open parking space, so he had to park two hundred meters away from the main gate. There is no aspect of the government health system he has not criticized ferociously. Then he talks about the incidents for several days.

He has been diagnosed with neurological diseases, a colon ulceration, an esophagus hernia, and a few other minor diseases.

DISEASES START IN THE MIND

As many medical practitioners and spiritual healers have declared, every disease has its root in the mind. Even genetic diseases have their triggers in the mind, without which they may remain dormant all the time. My friend is full of pain bodies. He provides space and opportunities for his ego to trigger them and puts them in his mind and emotions. He is always ready to resist the slightest off-standard incidents to flare and feed his ego.

All acts of inner resistance are negativity and work together. This negativity causes depression, resentment, and even potential suicidal despair.

The ego makes you believe that through resistance and negativity, things may start to work. It is the opposite: you make things go wrong wider and deeper. If you respond to the ego, it feeds on your response for another stronger round of attack.

The problem, as with my friend, is that when you identify with some form of negativity for an extended period of time, you become obsessed with it, and it sinks into the deeper unconscious level that you want to hold on to it. Any change would pose a threat to the identity you have created for yourself as an angry, depressed, and deprived person. In fact, you would do exactly the opposite and push away or even sabotage any positivity in your life to save your identity.

If you think you have this tendency of being compulsively resistive and negative, acknowledge it. Your ego may encourage you to deny it. This is what happens with my friend: when someone tells him to be positive, he claims that he has a high sense of positivity and that he is right in his evaluation of the incidents. This is a common phenomenon; it is also irrational.

Recurring resistance and negative reactions, such as severe illnesses and losses, will painfully offer messages for change and elevation in awareness and consciousness. But these changes should stem from changes in the level of consciousness, and that means coming to the present by doing conscious breathing and sense perception. When you break through the boundary of the presence, resistance and negativity have no role to play. If, for any reason, they persist, just remind yourself that you need to be more aware, more conscious, and more present.

MORE CHALLENGES FROM EGO

Your ego might challenge you more intensely now that you are somewhat aware and present. Continue reminding yourself to pay more attention and to be here and now. The presence will unfold with every attention call you give to yourself. Keep being aware and acknowledging, and do not allow any slight resistance or negativity to pile up by not being observant. Learn from the plants and animals. See how they stay in their present state, despite all the disturbances that happen around them. They have no ego to connect with and react to conditions that would not alter their state of being. You can do the same. Scratch the surface of the rock, and you will eventually reach the depth of it.

ONE PROBLEM

All the teachings of spirituality from all cultures, in their essence, suggest there is only one problem in the world, and there is only one solution to that problem. Although they use different words and terminologies, they all maintain that the state of unconsciousness of humanity is the only problem facing humanity. They all offer one solution: the consciousness of humanity. In between the problem and the solution, there is a world of explanations.

Every part of every teaching emphasizes severing the ties between consciousness and the downward pull of the ego. This process means relinquishing the attachment of the thoughts to what is not there, the past and the future. By implication, this means homecoming to the present time, the now. Where no problem or pain can exist, everything is amicable, amusing, and assured. People do not need to create the condition of consciousness; it is always there. They need to find the path to enter it.

How much more time do you think you need before you set yourself free of the pain and agony of staying unconscious? If you take more time, with it come more disruptions and unease.

If you leave the choice to your ego, it will undoubtedly take you deeper into an unconscious condition, which is madness. But consciousness is a natural state to which you are drawn. You must pour all your work into transmuting your mind into no-mind mindfulness, severing the ties to ego-induced thoughts. Until you endeavor to enter the realm of consciousness, you will involuntarily continue to suffer the consequences of the dysfunction of your mind-made torments. They happen to you because you are somewhere where you should not be, either the past or the future, where there is not enough presence and not enough light to shine on you.

The fact that you have chosen to read this book—or any similar book—is a momentous stride into your enlightenment. You will assuredly enjoy better times in the coming times, at the core of your divine existence.

RETENTION OF KNOWLEDGE

The retention of knowledge by reading is only 10 percent. Regular readers read a book more than once, which gives them extra retention. If you wish to increase your retention rate to 70 percent, discuss the content of the book with others. You can increase this rate to 80 percent by applying the knowledge learned and by rewriting or summarizing the content. The highest possible retention rate, 90 percent, occurs when you generalize the content and teach it to others.

I hope this book has helped you to live better times.

I hope you too help others.

If you wish to share your views about this book with me, kindly do so by email at Akbar-Jaffari@jafcon.com.

Printed in the United States
by Baker & Taylor Publisher Services